Military Medical Revolution

How the UK's Defence Medical Services transformed in conflict, 1990 – 2015

Colonel David Vassallo FRCSEd MA L/RAMC

Cover image 'In Safe Hands' (Medical Emergency Response Team in action aboard a CH47 Chinook above southern Afghanistan),
by Stuart Brown, oil on canvas, 2010. Courtesy of Stuart Brown, Skipper Press.
The original painting now hangs in the Royal College of Anaesthetists, London, United Kingdom.

Military Medical Revolution
How the UK's Defence Medical Services transformed in conflict, 1990–2015
by Colonel (Retd) David Vassallo FRCSEd MA L/RAMC

Author: David Vassallo. Any correspondence should be sent to: djvassallo@aol.com
Printed by Crest Publications, Kettering, UK. www.crestpublications.com
Designed and typeset by Ren Design Limited. renfree123@me.com

Author's Note

*'If anything positive can be said of war, it would be that it serves as a
catalyst for rapid improvements in medical understanding and care.'[1]*

This work is an analysis of the life-saving advances and transformation in military medicine catalysed by the post-Cold War conflicts of 1990 – 2015, especially those in Iraq and Afghanistan. It was originally produced as a dissertation under the title 'Military Medical Revolution, yes or no?' for the MA (History of Warfare) at King's College London, achieving Pass with Distinction in November 2015. It addressed the question: Do the advances in military medicine since 1990, with particular reference to the British Defence Medical Services, amount to a revolution in military medical affairs?

It is purposely published now, essentially unchanged except for some additional footnotes and illustrations, during a coronavirus pandemic which has seen the DMS mobilised to assist the NHS, but still at a time of relative peace when the DMS have not been actively involved in caring for large numbers of freshly wounded casualties for over five years. There are however plenty of conflicts elsewhere and, if history teaches us one thing, it is that this time of peace will be only a lull, and therefore a time to prepare, before the next war. In the meantime, experienced personnel are inevitably moving on and hard earned knowledge and lessons are in danger of being lost - as regrettably sometimes happened after previous wars - unless we ensure they are assimilated into doctrine, training and, crucially, into civilian and humanitarian trauma practice where globally the need is greatest. I am glad to see signs of this happening, but this is no time for complacency.

This overview therefore provides a benchmark, a set of standards, marking a pinnacle of achievement, against which to assess how well these lessons are being assimilated and what further progress is being made. It also points the way forward. It is intended to be a stimulus and inspiration for new practitioners of military medicine to continue to catalyse better trauma care worldwide.

A comment on footnotes: these follow the minimal wording house style of the War Studies Department, King's College London.
Full references are in the Bibliography.

---

1   Buckenmaier III & Mahoney, 2015, p.xxiii

Foreword

by Lieutenant General Louis Lillywhite
Master-General Army Medical Services and
Former Surgeon General UK Armed Forces

All wars, if of sufficient duration, lead to advances in medicine. David Vassallo argues in this book that in the current conflicts we have seen not just advances but a revolution. As evidence he cites the outcome, the "unexpected survivors", who are those that contemporary medicine considered unsavable.

He outlines the factors which support the use of the term "revolution", ranging from simple interventions at the point of wounding through exploitation of technological advances, to changes in concepts and doctrine. He highlights the fact that some of the developments were initially resisted, that the revolution arose from numerous developments which involved not just the medical services but the wider Armed Forces and drew on a variety of technological developments.

David's book highlights the names of many individuals who contributed to this revolution, but acknowledges there are many others who played their part, particularly in the USA, which space and time did not allow to be included. What is clear is that the advances almost exclusively originated from either the USA or UK and that from a UK perspective we owe a debt of gratitude to the USA for so freely co-operating with us to facilitate the simultaneous and timely adoption of many of the advances by UK and US Forces. He also highlights that other NATO nations contributed to the main UK hospital in Afghanistan and thereby also benefited from the UK/US advances.

David's final chapter addresses the future. I hope that the reader will consider to what extent we can emulate, at the beginning of a future conflict, the success which we achieved after some 20 plus years of the current conflicts. As he relates, many of the advances have or will become standard practice in the civilian environment and hopefully the "unexpected survivor" of today will become tomorrow's expected survivor. However, the conflict environment in which military medical services operate is far more hostile than a civilian one whilst all wars are different in numerous ways. We will need our future military medical services to once again adapt, as indeed they are doing in response to the current Covid-19 pandemic. This book demonstrates how it has been accomplished for the current conflicts. It is essential reading for today and tomorrow's clinical and military medical leaders.

Abstract
Military Medical Revolution, yes or no?

Do the advances in military medicine since 1990, with particular reference to the British Defence Medical Services, amount to a revolution in military medical affairs?

There have been many radical changes in British and Allied military medical concepts and doctrine, organisation and practice – together with many technological innovations – within recent years, especially the period 1990–2015. This period is marked at one end by the First Gulf War (Op GRANBY, 1990–1991) and the end of the Cold War, and at the other by cessation of combat operations in Afghanistan (Op HERRICK), and a primarily medical deployment to Sierra Leone (Op GRITROCK, 2014–2015).

This work first assesses how the criteria usually used to define a revolution in military affairs also apply to military medical affairs. Thereafter, it examines the key changes in the British military medical trauma system over this 25-year period, where necessary comparing with the US or NATO, and argues that these radical changes in the management of combat casualties, resulting in unprecedented survival and recovery rates, do indeed fulfil the criteria for a revolution in military medical affairs when assessed collectively.

It also explores the novel concept of collaborative powerhouses of revolution as a necessary form of organisational adaptation. These powerhouses are vitally important for sustaining revolution in between conflict, to ensure that lessons learned in war are remembered.

'Damage control surgery at Bastion' by Graeme Lothian, artist, reproduced with permission

Contents

Introduction

'In the last decade there has been a revolution in military medicine. We have totally changed the paradigm of how care is delivered, from pre-hospital, to hospital, to rehabilitation. There has been a revolution in the continuity of care, based on collaboration, co-operation instead of competition. Somehow we have managed to join the dots to get the sort of survival that we never dreamt we could possibly do.'[2]

Colonel Heidi Doughty, consultant in transfusion medicine, 2014

From Op GRANBY to Op GRITROCK, 1990–2015, from Quantity to Quality. There have been many radical changes in British (and Allied) military medical concepts and doctrine, organisation and practice – together with many technological innovations – within the last 25 years. This work will argue that these changes constitute a Revolution in Military Medical Affairs, this term being used interchangeably with 'military medical revolution'.

What were these changes that prompted Heidi Doughty, above, to declare that there has been a revolution in military medicine, and a change in the paradigm of care, and do they really meet recognised criteria for a revolution? What does this new paradigm signify for those critically injured in war and who now come under the care of Britain's Defence Medical Services (DMS)? Doughty gives two hints – collaboration, and the phenomenon of unexpected survivors.

This work will discuss the concepts of paradigm and revolution, then examine the key changes in British (and, where necessary, US or NATO) military medical concepts and doctrine, in medical technology, and in organisation and practice, that have occurred since the end of the Cold War and the First Gulf War (Op GRANBY, 1990 – 1991), with their emphasis on worst-case scenario planning. As my personal contribution to the literature, this work introduces the novel concept of powerhouses of revolution and, in examining how they interact with one another, argues how necessary they are to produce and sustain true revolution. This work will also argue that this revolution has had a wider impact, extending from the military into the civilian sphere, in the UK and globally.

After GRANBY, the DMS participated in small-scale interventions in the Balkans, Rwanda and Sierra Leone, before the momentous events of 9/11 propelled them into the crucible of an intense decade and more of bruising counter-insurgency conflict in Iraq and Afghanistan, where they transformed themselves completely to meet this challenge. After these conflicts they suddenly had to adapt again to combat an even deadlier foe, the Ebola virus in Sierra Leone (Op GRITROCK, 2014 – 2015).[3]

While researching this topic I came across the doctoral thesis by Timothy Hodgetts. He argued the case for revolution based on his own substantial contribution to combat casualty care.[4] I have adapted parts of his framework for this work. Much has been published since, across a wider range. Several other leading experts in combat casualty care, especially Lorne Blackbourne, Frank Butler, Brian Eastridge and John Holcomb, also documented revolutionary

---

2   Doughty, 2014

3   Bailey, et al, 2015, pp.1 – 7
4   Hodgetts, 2012a

changes from the US perspective.[5,6,7] Many people have contributed to transforming casualty care – there is space to highlight only a few.

Paradigm

The Oxford Dictionary defines a paradigm as: 'A world view underlying the theories and methodology of a particular scientific subject'.[8]

In 1962 Thomas Kuhn, in his seminal work 'The Structure of Scientific Revolution', challenged the commonly held evolutionary view of the nature of scientific progress: that science progressed steadily by the gradual accumulation of new ideas. Having reviewed many major scientific advances, Kuhn showed that science advanced the most by occasional revolutionary explosions of new knowledge, each revolution triggered by the introduction of new ways of thought so large that they must be called new paradigms, displacing the old.[9]

Kuhn used the term 'paradigm' for the core concepts underpinning a nascent revolution, thereby introducing it into general usage. A classic example of a new paradigm was the shift from the Ptolemaic view that the sun revolved around the earth to the Copernican understanding of the sun being the centre around which the earth rotated. Kuhn's seminal work led to the widespread adoption of the terms 'paradigm' and 'paradigm shift'.

Kuhn's concept of 'paradigm shift' is just as applicable to military medicine after 1990. The radical changes in practice and in trauma management systems, the explosion of research, new knowledge, and technological advances relating to the optimal management of critically wounded casualties were all triggered by a new paradigm that arose in the US in the late 1990s and was later defined by UK leaders in combat casualty care. This was the recognition and acceptance in doctrine and training that catastrophic haemorrhage, <C>, is the major killer on the battlefield, with its priority crystallised in the term <C>ABC (Catastrophic Haemorrhage, Airway, Breathing, Circulation).[10]

This 'paradigm shift' effectively resulted in a fundamental re-focusing of mind and effort onto the primacy of catastrophic haemorrhage, its physiology, its effects and its management – including preventive measures.

The previous paradigm of trauma care was instead characterised by ABC (Airway, Breathing and Circulation). This paradigm had arisen in 1976 in the context of civilian trauma practice in the US (where blunt trauma is much more common than penetrating trauma – the polar opposite to the situation on a battlefield). The ABC concept led to the creation of the Advanced Trauma Life Support (ATLS) system with its structured approach to trauma. ATLS was adopted by the American College of Surgeons in 1977; the ATLS course rapidly became compulsory for American clinicians (military and civilian), and eventually became the gold standard for trauma management worldwide.[11]

5   Blackbourne, et al, 2012a, pp.S372 – S377
6   Blackbourne, et al, 2012b, pp.S378 – S387
7   Blackbourne, et al, 2012c, pp.S388 – S394
8   Oxford Dictionary, 2015
9   Kuhn, 1962

10   Hodgetts, et al, 2006, pp.745 – 746
11   Carmont, 2005, pp.87 – 91

ATLS taught that Airway obstruction and Breathing problems had precedence over Circulation (haemorrhage), with clinicians being directed to ignore ongoing haemorrhage until they had excluded A or B problems. This was based on the premise that a patient with airway obstruction would die sooner than a patient suffering from haemorrhage.

This was counter-intuitive to clinicians with actual battlefield experience. Unfortunately, this ABC paradigm, having evolved within civilian practice, took insufficient account of the relative frequency of life-threatening injuries actually sustained on the battlefield, where haemorrhage is overwhelmingly the most common problem. It would be some 20 years before this anomalous situation was openly acknowledged in the US military, in the aftermath of the Battle of Mogadishu in 1993,[12] and it would take the shock of large numbers of casualties in Iraq from 2004 onwards to consolidate the paradigm shift to <C>ABC.

Revolution in military affairs: the debate

The Pentagon's forward-thinking Director of the Office of Net Assessment, and a veteran of the RAND Corporation, **Andrew Marshall**, sparked off the RMA debate in the States immediately after the 1990 – 1991 Gulf War.[13,14] He identified that a revolution in military affairs was occurring, and moved beyond the Soviet focus on technology, stating:

'**Technology** makes possible the revolution, but the revolution itself takes place only when **new concepts of operation** develop and, in many cases, **new military organisations** are created'. [15] [my emphasis]

Andrew Krepinevich, now President of the Center for Strategic and Budgetary Assessments, worked as an analyst for Marshall at the time. He developed a succinct definition for this emerging revolution:

'It is what occurs when the application of **new technologies** into a significant number of **military systems** combines with **innovative operational concepts** and **organisational adaptations** in a way that fundamentally alters the character and conduct of conflict'.[16] [my emphasis]

Colin Gray, Professor of International Politics and Strategic Studies at the University of Reading, preferred a truly minimalist definition, variously defining a RMA as:

'a radical change in the character **or** conduct of war',[17] and
'a radical change in the character **and** conduct of war'.[18] [my emphasis]

Eliot Cohen, now Robert E. Osgood Professor of Strategic Studies at Johns Hopkins University, stipulated three tests to judge whether a revolution has actually occurred:

- Do military forces look fundamentally different from what they were in the past?
- Are the processes of battle different?
- Are outcomes also different?[19]

12   Butler, et al, 1996, pp.3 – 16
13   Freedman, 2013, p.215
14   Rosen, 2010, pp.469 – 482
15   Marshall, 1993, p.1

16   Krepinevich, 1994, p.30
17   Gray, 2005, p.105
18   Gray, 2006, p.vi
19   Cohen, 2004, p.403

The RMA debate gradually evolved (transformed!) into a debate on transformation, into how militaries innovate and adapt in war. Four key factors identified as being necessary for transformation are:

- Organisational interests (particularly of the government or party in power)
- New ideas (most effective when championed from the top)
- Leadership
- Feedback from operational experience[20]

It is the militaries engaged in long wars or defeated in war who are generally most motivated to learn from operational experience, with time enabling them to adapt effectively to changing circumstances and to innovate, for instance by developing new technologies or concepts to meet operational challenges.[21]

Organisational (political) interests are particularly important when casualties begin to be sustained in conflict, especially if the conflict is controversial, as in Iraq (2003), widely denounced as an 'unjust war'. No politician or general wants to be perceived as not caring about the wounded, or to be seen as delaying the procurement of life-saving equipment. This may explain why high-profile projects (such as introducing CT scanners to deployed hospitals, p.24) are more likely to be successful if initiated during conflict.

The other key factors for transformation (championing of new ideas, leadership, and feedback from operational experience) will be emphasised throughout this work.

Revolution in military medical affairs

Casualties are inevitable in war. Caring for these casualties is the raison d'etre of military medicine. Military medicine necessarily responds to changes in the character or conduct of war, particularly where weaponry and wounding mechanisms are concerned, adapting to meet these new challenges and innovating accordingly.

If one can recognise a revolution in military affairs, what then constitutes a revolution in military medical affairs? Or a transformation in military medicine?

Timothy Hodgetts, who specialised in emergency medicine and became Director of the UK's Joint Medical Command, focused his thesis on his own contribution to revolution. He adapted Gray's definition to characterise a revolution in military medical affairs as:

'A radical change in the character or practice of military medicine'.[22]

Hodgetts also adapted Cohen's three tests to judge whether a revolution has actually occurred, by placing them into a medical setting:

- Do military [medical] forces look fundamentally different?
- Are the processes of 'battle' different?
- Are [clinical] outcomes different?[23]

20   Farrell, 2013a, p.3
21   Farrell, 2013b, pp.1 – 23
22   Hodgetts, 2012a, pp.24 – 25
23   Hodgetts, 2012a, p.28

For this work, I shall use Cohen's criteria as adapted by Hodgetts to judge revolution. The most crucial of Cohen's criteria is his last one, the clinical outcomes, as it is the casualty who is at the heart of war and military medicine, who survives or not, or recovers fully or partially. These outcomes are measurable.

I shall also adapt the various definitions of revolution, above, to subtly incorporate the concept of collaborative powerhouses, as follows:

A revolution in military medical affairs occurs when new technologies applied throughout the military trauma system combine with dramatic doctrinal changes, innovative operational concepts and collaborative organisational adaptations to cause a radical change in the character and practice of military medicine.

This work will deal with each of the main areas in this definition. It will show how each key change catalyses another, or acts synergistically.

Powerhouses of revolution

While revolutionary ideas may originate with one individual, this work will argue that, for revolution to take hold, it is necessary to develop a critical mass of committed individuals in several centres (the powerhouse concept), all working towards the same goal but through different approaches. Most importantly, they must collaborate – the end result then being what Heidi Doughty, p.6, recognised as happening in this last decade.[24]

Several medical powerhouses have risen to the fore in recent years, innovative centres of excellence in different fields (from training through to rehabilitation and research) with highly motivated individuals and natural leaders, which each adapted to the operational challenges imposed by high-intensity conflict in Iraq and Afghanistan, and which came together synergistically to drive revolution. Such powerhouses developed mainly, but not exclusively, in the US and UK, and collaborated nationally and internationally to catalyse change.

This work will examine the role of some of the main UK powerhouses, while concentrating on one, Bastion Hospital in Helmand Province, Afghanistan, because of its particular legacy. Importantly, while Bastion Hospital is no longer, the other powerhouses continue to work together post-Afghanistan, in preparation for future conflict.

Methodology

The literature on military medical transformation focuses on doctrinal and conceptual changes, technological innovations, and on organisational and operational adaptations. Chapters 1 to 3 will examine these three themes. Chapter 3 will also explore the concept of 'powerhouses of revolution' as a crucial form of organisational adaptation. It will argue that this concept is fundamental to the genesis of military medical revolution and very probably other revolutions, and it is critical for the sustainability of revolution in the absence of the driver of ongoing conflict. Chapter 4 will focus on sustaining revolution in between conflict.

---

24   Doughty, 2014

Chapter 1: Doctrinal and Conceptual Revolution

This chapter will examine the recently developed concepts that influence combat casualty care from point of wounding through to aeromedical evacuation to the UK. The following diagram illustrates how these concepts have been integrated doctrinally to form the current system of military medical care, a continuum now known in the DMS as the Operational Patient Care Pathway.[25,26,27]

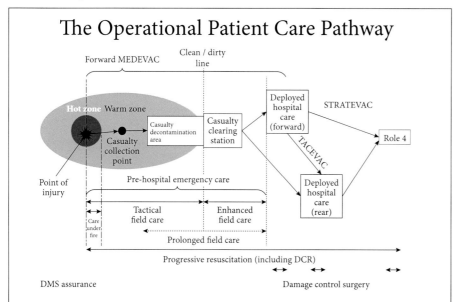

The Operational Patient Care Pathway

---

25 Operational Patient Care Pathway, 2014
26 Bricknell, 2014, pp.164–169
27 Allied Joint Publication-4.10(B), 2015, p.(1)5

Bastion Hospital in Afghanistan is represented in this diagram by 'Deployed Hospital Care (Forward)' and the Royal Centre for Defence Medicine (RCDM), and subsequent rehabilitation in the UK, is represented by Role 4.[28] Many of these concepts stem from a paradigm shift in combat casualty care.

Paradigm shift – catastrophic haemorrhage, ABC to <C>ABC

This paradigm shift was the recognition in the late 1990s that catastrophic haemorrhage, <C>, was the major killer on the battlefield. This was formalised doctrinally in the UK in 2005, shortly before British troops deployed into Helmand and while conflict was ongoing in Iraq,[29] and will be discussed further in the next section. It was to underpin every aspect of combat casualty care in both theatres and beyond, in military and in civilian practice.

Care on the battlefield

'My friends from the Regiment all rushed in, even though it was a suspected minefield. They worked to give me first aid on the ground. A young team medic put a surgical airway into my trachea (to help my breathing), which was something that he'd never done before. There is absolutely no question that saved my life.'

Lance Bombardier Ben Parkinson, injured by anti-tank mine, 2006.[30]

---

28 Operational Patient Care Pathway (Figures), 2014
29 Hodgetts, et al, 2006, pp.745–746
30 Parkinson, 2013, pp.78–83

Most fatalities occur in the first minutes after injury, so first aid delivered at the point of wounding is fundamental to improving survival rates. It is here that many of the recent transformational practices in military medicine have occurred. This section compares developments in UK 'Pre-hospital Emergency Care' with US 'Tactical Combat Casualty Care', as the tide of change sometimes flowed one way, sometimes the other, across the pond. Helicopter-borne care is discussed under 'En-route Care'.

(UK) Pre-hospital Emergency Care

Team Medic

Parkinson, quoted above, survived because a team medic inserted a surgical airway in the 'platinum 10 minutes' after he was injured. Most pre-hospital deaths occur in this period, when usually the only access to care is by fellow soldiers, who normally work in small teams of four to eight. This led to the vital concept of 'Team Medics' in 2006, giving at least one soldier in four extra medical training and equipment for life-saving manoeuvres.[31,32] This built on the 'buddy system' first developed by US Special Forces in Vietnam.[33] The average time for Team Medics to start treatment is now two minutes after injury. This transformed the survival rates before soldiers receive specialist care, and as a result NATO changed its doctrine in 2010 to ensure effective first aid is provided within those first 10 minutes.[34,35]

Battlefield Advanced Trauma Life Support (BATLS)

Advanced Trauma Life Support was introduced to the UK in 1988 by Colonel **Ian Haywood** (Professor of Military Surgery, and a pioneer of pre-hospital care), after he attended an ATLS course in the States.[36] Haywood created a military version of the course, initially named 'British Army Trauma Life Support'. This soon evolved in response to triservice training needs to become 'Battlefield Advanced Trauma Life Support' (BATLS).[37] Haywood's philosophy was that any military doctor, irrespective of specialty, should be able to sustain the seriously injured for the first 'golden' hour after injury, usually enough time to get to hospital.[38]

BATLS earned its laurels in the 1991 Gulf War, and proved its worth in mass casualty situations in the Balkan conflicts.[39,40] BATLS continues to be taught to all military doctors, and has been extended to nurses and combat medical technicians under the name 'Battlefield Advanced Resuscitation Training Skills' (BARTS).

BATLS has undergone four major revisions to incorporate developments in civilian and military trauma resuscitation practice and to reflect best practice from operational experience. The most significant revision was in 2005, when it incorporated the new <C>ABC paradigm, and became much more interactive.[41]

31   British Army website. Casualty Care http://www.army.mod.uk/welfare-support/23238.aspx (25 July 2015)

32   Hodgetts & Findlay, 2012b, pp.162–170

33   Hamblen, 2012, pp.536–43

34   NATO, 2010

35   Allied Joint Publication-4.10(B), 2015, p.(1)17

36   Payne, 1995, pp.71–72

37   BATLS 2008, pp.2–3

38   BASICS website. http://www.basics.org.uk/about_us/imc_greats/haywood_bio (5 July 2015).

39   Riley & Mahoney, 1996, pp.542–546

40   Vassallo, et al, 1998, pp.61–66

41   Hodgetts, et al, 2005

BATLS 2005 also introduced a stepwise approach to trauma resuscitation, with increasingly sophisticated treatment delivered at four levels of care, namely care under fire, tactical field care, field resuscitation (team-based resuscitation at Role 1) and advanced resuscitation (consultant led, within a Role 2 or Role 3 hospital facility). The concepts of care under fire and tactical field care were borrowed from US Tactical Combat Casualty Care. BATLS has been accepted as the gold standard military pre-hospital course for NATO and Sweden,[42] being co-ordinated through the Interallied Confederation of Medical Reserve Officers.[43] The first NATO nation to adopt BATLS was the Czech Republic, after the BATLS care its soldiers received in Bosnia during a helicopter crash in 1998 sparked off a unique chain of multinational medical co-operation.[44]

(US) Tactical Combat Casualty Care (TCCC)

Until the disastrous Battle of Mogadishu in October 1993, in which 19 American servicemen were killed, US battlefield pre-hospital trauma care had followed exactly the same ATLS guidelines developed for the urban US environment.[45] ATLS philosophy laid emphasis on 'ABC': Airway, Breathing and Circulation. Being a civilian course, it took no account of the operational environment. Despite this, all US military physicians aiming to accredit in trauma management had to undertake this course and follow its philosophy. Following Mogadishu, the US Special Operations Command initiated a study into the conduct of combat casualty care. This two-year study, conducted by two physicians with special operations experience, US Navy Captain Frank Butler and Lieutenant Colonel John Hagmann, concluded that conventional

civilian trauma medicine, as taught in ATLS, was not appropriate for casualty care within the tactical environment, especially when care has to be given under fire.[46]

Butler and Hagmann issued TCCC guidelines for optimising casualty care during tactical operations, dividing the stages of care into three phases: 'care under fire', rendered while still under effective enemy fire; 'tactical field care', rendered once no longer under effective enemy fire; and 'combat casualty evacuation care', rendered once the casualty has been picked up by aircraft, vehicle or boat. These TCCC guidelines have been regularly updated ever since 1996. They now underpin all pre-hospital trauma care carried out by US Forces,[47] and have been adopted by several other NATO nations.[48] The wheel has come full circle, for US civilian trauma services have now adopted the precepts of TCCC for blast and penetrating trauma.[49]

Tourniquets – yes, no, or how?

'The prompt use of a tourniquet will frequently be of life-saving importance. It is useful chiefly in controlling haemorrhage when great vessels of the extremities are injured. Usually this is in the presence of a compound fracture or amputation. Since tourniquets introduce hazards of ischemia and serious nerve damage, their use is to be as infrequent as possible and for as short a time as possible.'

Henry Beecher, 1951.[50]

42 Lundberg, et al, 2008, pp.34 – 37
43 CIOMR website http://ciomr.org/service/resources/militmilitary-trauma-care/battlefield-advanced-trauma-life-support-batls/ (12 August 2015)
44 Vassallo, et al, 1999, pp.7 – 12
45 Carmont, 2005, pp.87 – 91

46 Butler, et al, 1996, pp.3 – 16
47 Gerhardt, et al, 2015
48 Savage, et al, 2011, pp.S118–S123
49 Smith, 2014
50 Beecher, 1951, p.195

The conceptual shift from using tourniquets as a last resort to their becoming a universal first aid measure has arguably been the pre-hospital medical breakthrough of the wars in Afghanistan and Iraq.[51]

The risk to life of uncontrolled haemorrhage has been intuitively understood in all wars, but the use of tourniquets to control compressible limb haemorrhage, while usually recognised as saving lives, has always been attended by controversy.[52] Beecher, above, illustrates the dilemma. The perceived risks of using tourniquets, especially if applied incorrectly, often militated against their use. As a result, during the Vietnam War, when tourniquet use was actively discouraged, some 2,500 soldiers died of isolated limb haemorrhage for want of a tourniquet.[53]

One controversial recommendation by Butler and Hagmann in their 1996 TCCC guidelines was to reintroduce tourniquets for extremity haemorrhage. This precept found favour with the special operations community, though the lack of effective tourniquets hampered their introduction.[54-55]

Soon after the onset of conflict in Afghanistan (2001) and Iraq (2003), when some US soldiers died of potentially compressible limb haemorrhage, various designs underwent urgent testing. The turning point came after Congressional pressure in 2005, when Army Surgeon General Kevin Kiley mandated that the Combat Application Tourniquet should become standard individual issue to deploying US service personnel, replacing the ineffective Second World War tourniquets in medical stocks.[56] Every soldier soon had a

tourniquet and was trained in its use, in time for the surge in sectarian violence in Iraq.[57] By 2012, approximately 2,000 US military lives had been saved by tourniquets.[58]

Building on TCCC precepts and a critical appraisal of UK and US conflict experience, Hodgetts *et al* formalised the underpinning concept of <C>ABC, introducing it into UK doctrine (and into BATLS training) in time for the Combat Application Tourniquet to be issued to individual soldiers for the initial Helmand deployment in 2006.

There was initial resistance to this from senior military orthopaedic surgeons, who argued against tourniquet use on grounds that would have been familiar to Beecher.[59,60,61] With rapidly accruing evidence of safety if used correctly, by 2008 tourniquets were no longer the most controversial item in combat casualty care, and the emphasis had shifted to how and when they should be used.[62]

51   Kragh, *et al*, 2013, pp.5 – 25
52   Kragh, et al, 2012, pp.242 – 252
53   Maughon, 1970, pp.8 – 13
54   Butler, et al, 2007, pp.1 – 19
55   Butler & Blackbourne, 2012, pp.S395 – S402
56   Kragh, et al, 2013, pp.5 – 25

57   PHTLS, 2005
58   Kragh, et al, 2013, pp.5 – 25
59   Parker & Clasper, 2007, pp.10 – 12
60   Hodgetts & Mahoney, 2007a, pp.12 – 15
61   Brodie, et al, 2007, pp.310 – 313
62   Kragh, et al, 2012, pp.242 – 252

En-route Care – Medical Emergency Response Team (MERT)

'Then the Chinook helicopter came in to try and get me. It was a huge relief to see it, but then a rocket-propelled grenade was fired at it ... so it withdrew and circled overhead. That's when I thought, "I'm actually going to die here."... Then the Apache turned up, and rained fire down on the location ... so that the Chinook could come back in and land.'

Private Alex Stringer.[63]

Private Alex Stringer was blown up by an improvised explosive device (IED) in Afghanistan on 19 January 2011. He is a triple amputee and 'unexpected survivor' – owing his life to the Medical Emergency Response Team (MERT) on board that Chinook.

The pivotal link between casualties on the battlefields of Helmand and the hospital at Camp Bastion was the iconic helicopter-borne MERT based at Bastion, as the danger of IEDs largely precluded road evacuation (fortunately, air superiority was not an issue).

The MERT was a revolutionary concept, taking the most experienced healthcare professionals (a consultant in anaesthesia or emergency medicine, a nurse and two paramedics) directly to the most critically wounded on the battlefield. It had its precedents in the helicopter-borne Incident Response Teams of the 1990s, which carried an anaesthetist and operating department practitioner to the scene of injury.[64]

In Safe Hands (MERT in action aboard a CH47 Chinook over southern Afghanistan)[65]

MERT was introduced on Op HERRICK 4 in 2006, utilising the skills of clinicians already deployed to Bastion and the Royal Air Force's sturdy and spacious CH-47 Chinook helicopter.[66-67] From 2007, in-flight advanced resuscitation included blood transfusion, a critical life-saving innovation.[68] Anaesthetists or emergency physicians were deployed specifically for the MERT from 2008 onwards.[69]

---

63 Stringer, 2013, pp.26 – 35
64 Vassallo, et al, 2005, pp.19 – 29

65 Stuart Brown, artist. Reproduced with permission, http://skipperpress.com/portfolio/gallery-prints/in-safe-hands-2/ (23 August 2015).
66 Davis, et al, 2006
67 Davis, et al, 2007, pp.269 – 273
68 Nicholson Roberts & Berry, 2012, pp.186 – 189
69 Pope, 2015, pp.44 – 46

The MERT was preferentially tasked with evacuating the most severely injured casualties. The wisdom of this intuitive measure was borne out when the outcomes of casualties retrieved by MERT were compared with those retrieved by the smaller US Army DUSTOFF and US Air Force PEDRO helicopters (which only carried paramedics).[70-71] The physician-led MERT capability transported a higher percentage of severely injured casualties, while achieving greater than predicted survival.

Casualties transported by MERT also had their surgery earlier, having been better resuscitated en route. This alone made the difference between life and death for many casualties, probably accounting for some unexpected survivors.[72]

Damage control resuscitation

'The view of the consultants, US as well as British, supported by feedback from the UK Joint Trauma Clinical Case Conference, was that the very aggressive Damage Control Resuscitation paradigm employed in Bastion Hospital was continuing to pay dividends in terms of unexpected survival.'

Colonel Peter Gilbert, Commanding Officer, Bastion Hospital, 2010.[73]

The radical changes in trauma management over this last decade are based on new insights into the pathophysiology of coagulopathy and haemorrhage.

The concept of damage control resuscitation (DCR) was introduced into the British Defence Medical Services in 2007 to draw a range of advances in pre-hospital and hospital-based military trauma care together into a coherent doctrine,[74-75] now fully integrated with NATO.[76]

DCR is defined as 'a systemic approach to major trauma combining the <C>ABC paradigm with a series of clinical techniques from point of wounding to definitive treatment in order to minimise blood loss, maximise tissue oxygenation and optimise outcome.[77]

Damage Control Resuscitation, Bastion Hospital.[78]

70 Apodaca, et al, 2013, pp.S157–S163
71 Morrison, et al, 2013a, pp.330–334
72 *Ibid.*
73 Gilbert, 2010, p.2

74 Hodgetts, et al, 2007b, pp.299–300
75 Tarmey, et al, 2012, pp.S417–S422
76 Allied Joint Publication-4.10(B), 2015
77 Hodgetts, et al, 2007b, pp.299–300
78 Gora Pathak, orthopaedic surgeon and artist. With permission

Specifically, DCR encompasses haemostasis techniques from point of wounding (topical haemostatic agents; tourniquet); BATLS interventions; advanced in-flight intervention by the MERT (induction of anaesthesia, thoracostomy [drainage of blood from the chest] and blood transfusion); a consistently consultant-based trauma team at the field hospital (rapid decision making); an aggressive approach to coagulopathy, hypothermia and acidosis in the Emergency Department ('haemostatic resuscitation'); diagnostic imaging support and damage control radiology; and damage control surgery.[79]

Damage control surgery consists of three phases: an abbreviated operation (limited to under one hour) concentrating on haemorrhage and intestinal leakage control (not repair), a period in intensive care to correct the lethal triad of coagulopathy, acidosis and hypothermia, and a return to surgery for definitive repair. This concept is now fully embraced by trauma clinicians, and is integral to DCR, in the context of 'surgery is part of resuscitation'.[80]

The integration of DCR into doctrine also assists in siting medical facilities to ensure that casualties receive prompt surgical attention within accepted timelines.[81,82] NATO medical services now aim to give enhanced first aid within the first 10 minutes (the 'platinum 10 minutes'); to start advanced resuscitation within an hour (the 'golden hour'); and to undertake the first surgery preferably within one hour, but no later than two.[83]

Haemostatic resuscitation

'Transmission of positive experience ("Give whole blood when blood is lost") requires laborious effort, and one looks around for easier ways out.'

Henry Beecher, 1951.[84]

The proactive management of the recently recognised bleeding disorder associated with trauma (Coagulopathy of Trauma shock) is known as haemostatic resuscitation, and incorporates massive blood transfusion (defined as the infusion of 10 or more units of blood within 24 hours, or over four units within one hour) according to defined protocols.[85] This process has evolved so radically in recent years, and now differing so much from original ATLS practice, that it amounts to a paradigm change in transfusion practice.

A Massive Transfusion Protocol has been incorporated into UK military medical doctrine since 2007, when it was introduced into Iraq and Afghanistan.[86]

The massive transfusion process for casualties with catastrophic haemorrhage now includes pre-emptive component therapy, with the early use of plasma and platelets in a 1:1:1 ratio with packed red blood cell concentrates (the ratio approximating that in whole blood). This has been shown to improve survival.[87]

79   Midwinter, 2009, pp.323 – 326
80   Lamb, et al, 2014, pp.242 – 249
81   Tai, et al, 2009b, pp.253 – 256
82   Gilbert, 2013, p.11
83   Allied Joint Publication-4.10(B), 2015, p.(1)17

84   Beecher, 1951, pp.193 – 200
85   Doughty, et al, 2011, pp.S277 – S283
86   Russell, 2012, pp.(8)21 – 23
87   Doughty, et al, 2011, pp.S277 – S283

Warm fresh whole blood, collected from pre-screened emergency donor panels and stored warm for up to 24 hours, is being used increasingly often instead of component therapy for ongoing haemorrhage and in isolated combat units.[88,89,90]

This lesson was learned in the First World War, where an infusion of a single unit of direct donor-to-recipient fresh whole blood became the norm for patients in severe shock,[91] and again in the Second World War with its far forward field transfusion units, but was largely forgotten afterwards with the move to component therapy, as was predicted by Beecher, above.

Right turn resuscitation

'They took me to Camp Bastion, the field hospital, which took about twenty minutes. Once I reached it, they took me directly into the operating theatre and the last thing I remember was a nurse talking to me. She said to me, "Derek, be strong, you're going to be OK".'

Private Derek Derenalagi.[92]

The above is a personal account of 'right turn resuscitation' by Derek Derenalagi, blown up by an IED in Helmand Province on 19 July 2007, suffering a bilateral through-thigh amputation, and classified as an unexpected survivor. The pithy phrase 'right turn resuscitation', introduced at Bastion in

2007,[93] perfectly epitomises the new 'damage control resuscitation – damage control surgery' philosophy that saved Derenalagi's life. It is the process whereby critically unstable casualties bypass the emergency room altogether, going right into the operating theatre for surgical control of haemorrhage, followed by rapid imaging ('damage control radiology'), ongoing resuscitation and a short period of ITU stabilisation. The casualty would then usually return to theatre for further damage control surgery. Colonel Peter Mahoney describes it eloquently in *Have you heard of MASH?* [94]

Importantly, the phrase 'right turn resuscitation' is firmly rooted within the concept of Bastion as a powerhouse that has catalysed a transformation in combat casualty care.[95]

The 'right turn' reflected the geographical location of the Bastion theatres to the right of the emergency department, but its ethos symbolises taking the right decision for the right patient at the right time followed by the right response.[96,97]

Aeromedical evacuation – Critical Care Air Support Team (CCAST)

After resuscitation and surgery in the field hospital, the next crucial link in the evacuation chain of casualties is strategic aeromedical evacuation to a Role 4 hospital in the home country. For British casualties from Iraq and Afghanistan, this is the Royal Centre for Defence Medicine, now situated at the Queen Elizabeth Hospital, Birmingham.

88   Hess, *et al*, 2008, pp.9 – 10
89   Davies, 2015, doi:10.1136/jramc-2015-000413
90   Beckett, et al, 2015, pp.S153 – S156
91   Boulton & Roberts, 2014, pp.325 – 334
92   Derenelagi, 2013, pp.186 – 193

93   Tai & Russell, 2011, pp.S310 – S314
94   Mahoney, 2010, pp.16 – 18
95   Vassallo, 2015c, doi:10.1136/jramc-2015-000465
96   Vassallo, 2014, pp.16 – 21
97   Vassallo, 2015b, pp.160 – 166

The paradigm shift in strategic aeromedical capability and doctrine occurred after the debacle of Mogadishu in 1993, where the surge of casualties overwhelmed medical resources. Until then, the US and UK aeromedical systems were geared towards evacuating stable casualties from theatre, relying on specialists and equipment from field hospitals to accompany critically ill casualties. This presented a serious logistic challenge to these hospitals that could ill afford to lose capability.

US experience

Mogadishu provided the spur for transformation, leading the US to establish the Critical Care Air Transport Team (CCATT) programme in 1994, consisting of teams with a critical care physician, critical care nurse, and respiratory therapist, with supplies and equipment, to create a rapidly deployable mobile intensive care unit to evacuate unstable casualties safely, even within hours of surgery.[98]

This radical change in capability allowed the US military medical system to adjust doctrine in response to changing strategy, as the Cold War concept of caring for multiple casualties in large hospitals in-theatre morphed into expeditionary operations with limited medical holding capability. Politically, after the 1993 debacle, such missions could not be undertaken without the safety net of the CCATT capability.[99] The same would apply to the UK. Thus, soon after 9/11, the level of care provided by CCATT was such that combat casualties were safely evacuated within four hours of their arrival at a British field hospital in Bagram, Afghanistan, with three casualties having had surgery in the meantime.[100]

The Iraq and Afghanistan conflicts provided the first wide-scale test of the CCATT concept and capabilities. A review of the CCATT programme over a decade of operations showed it contributed materially to the striking improvement in combat casualty survival, and the unprecedented success and attendant minimal mortality of movement of CCATT patients has been described as a paradigm shift for trauma surgery doctrine.[101]

UK experience

The UK military similarly developed analogous Critical Care Air Support Teams (CCAST) in the 1990s,[102] under the control of the RAF's Tactical Medical Wing.

CCAST capabilities have improved steadily since Op GRANBY, with expansion in medical and nursing staffing levels, and enhancements to equipment. Each CCAST now consists of two flight nurses trained in intensive care, a medical devices technician, a consultant anaesthetist, and a flight nursing assistant.[103] In essence, the CCAST provides a mobile intensive care capability for the British armed forces and entitled civilians wherever they serve overseas. By the end of Op HERRICK (2014), some 4,500 casualties had been evacuated by CCAST to the UK.[104]

No rigorous review of CCAST has been published. While it would be extremely challenging to identify the contribution of CCAST alone within the overall UK military trauma system, the latest evidence on improved survival of complex polytrauma casualties from Iraq and Afghanistan suggests that CCAST has contributed materially to this.[105]

98   Rice, et al, 2008, p.207
99   Tipping, et al, 2015, pp.391 – 399
100 Vassallo, et al, 2003, pp.47 – 52

101 Ingalls, et al, 2014, pp.807 – 813
102 Patterson, et al, 2014, pp.1005 – 1012
103 Turner, et al, 2009, pp.171 – 174
104 Vassallo, 2015c, doi:10.1136/jramc-2015-000465
105 Penn-Barwell, et al, 2015, pp.1014 – 1020

The Quiet Battle (CCAST in action aboard C-130 Hercules)[106]

Summary

This chapter has described the paradigm shifts and new concepts that have transformed combat casualty care since the end of the Cold War. They have resulted in radically new doctrine, prompting new technologies and requiring new processes.

The next chapter will focus on the technological innovations that have been introduced throughout the military trauma system.

---

106   Donald MacDonald, artist. http://www.donaldmacdonaldspaintings.co.uk/id24.html (28 June 2015)

Chapter 2:
Technological Revolution

Definitions of revolution all include technological innovations, applied system-wide. These underwrite and enable revolution. This chapter will focus on those that have impacted most on survival or functional recovery.

Haemorrhage control

The focus of much innovation in military medicine has been on pre-hospital haemorrhage control. The crucial factor is whether haemorrhage is externally compressible (from pelvis and extremities, controllable by binders, tourniquets and dressings), internal and non-compressible (within abdomen and thorax, requiring surgery), or junctional (groins, neck and axillae, not amenable to tourniquets, but potentially to haemostatic dressings or clamping).

Pelvic binders

Open pelvic fractures, commonly associated with IED injuries, cause massive haemorrhage that is amenable to circumferential compression. In the last 15 years, effective compression devices have been developed, such as the SAM Pelvic Sling. Their use is life-saving in the pre-hospital setting.[107]

Tourniquets

The revival of this concept was covered in Chapter 1. Once Combat Application Tourniquets were widely introduced into US (2005) and then UK practice (2006),[108] evidence of their safety accrued in the Joint Theatre Trauma Registries, and soon in the medical literature.[109] The accumulated results of their use through a decade of war, during which injury severity rose steadily and tourniquet requirement rates rose tenfold, show conclusively that tourniquets, when used correctly, have saved many lives.[110]

Compression dressings

The Israeli Elastic First Field Dressing replaced the standard UK military field dressing in 2005, being easier to use and more effective in controlling extremity haemorrhage.[111]

Haemostatic dressings

Junctional vascular injuries constitute some of the most difficult challenges on the battlefield. It was this injury, depicted graphically in the book *Black Hawk Down*,[112] that killed a Ranger in Mogadishu in 1993, and that spurred the development of topical haemostatic dressings. The first effective one was *QuikClot*®, zeolite powder derived from volcanic dust, introduced by the US in 2003.[113] This was followed by chitosan, derived from crushed shellfish,

---

107   Brown, *et al*, 2012, pp.536–43

108   Brodie, et al, 2007, pp.310 – 313
109   Kragh, et al, 2013, pp.5 – 25
110   Kragh, et al, 2015, pp.184 – 90
111   Brown, et al, 2012, pp.536 – 43
112   Bowden, 1999, pp.209 – 245
113   Rhee, et al, 2008, pp.1093 – 1099

impregnated into a bandage as *HemCon®*, introduced in 2006.[114] Both products were superseded when *Celox Gauze®* (Combat Gauze), pliable ribbon gauze impregnated with a chitosan-like product,[115] entered UK practice in 2010.[116]

Other measures used in attempts to control junctional haemorrhage include clamps or compression devices, such as the *Combat Ready Clamp®* approved by the US Food and Drug Administration in 2010,[117] but their effectiveness remains unproven.[118,119] What they do indicate is a willingness to innovate in the face of operational challenge, coupled with organisational support.

Transfusion advances

'The shock we saw was caused by blood loss … it was cured by blood administration'.

Henry Beecher, 1947.[120]

'The use of the Massive Transfusion Protocol … crossed unexpected boundaries with a casualty surviving following transfusion in theatre of an astounding 274 units of blood and blood products …'

Colonel Peter Gilbert, Commanding Officer, Bastion Hospital, 2010.[121]

The First World War saw the first effective use of blood transfusion,[122] and one of the most important developments from the Spanish Civil War and Second World War was the widespread provision of blood transfusion far forward, with self-contained mobile field transfusion units.[123,124]

This work argues that the Afghanistan conflict saw equally radical advances in transfusion practice, exemplified by Gilbert's quote above. The paradigm change here was in massive transfusion management (see Chapter 1).

The relevant developments at Bastion Hospital were:

2007 – Massive Transfusion Protocol[125]

2008 – Operational platelet apheresis introduced by Heidi Doughty (it had never before been possible to provide platelets on operations)

2008 – Pre-hospital transfusion by MERT

2009 – Laboratory Information Management System with full barcoding (this transformed the speed and accuracy of delivering large amounts of blood components)

2009 – Rotational Thromboelastometry (ROTEM) (this 'by-the-bedside' technique measured platelet function and clotting factor deficiencies, optimising haemostasis management).[126]

114   Wedmore, et al, 2006, pp.655 – 658
115   Kozen, et al, 2008, pp.74 – 81
116   Russell, 2012, pp.(3)19 – 21
117   Blackbourne, et al, 2012a, pp.S372 – S377
118   CADTH, 2014, pp.1 – 12
119   Walker, et al, 2014, pp.1585 – 1589
120   Beecher, et al, 1947, p.676
121   Gilbert, 2010, p.2

122   Robertson, 1918, pp.759 – 762
123   Stewart & Majada, 2014
124   Parker, et al, 2015, pp.2 – 4
125   Surgeon General's Policy Letter, 2007
126   Jansen, et al, 2014, pp.154 – 61

Associated advances were in cannulation techniques, particularly intraosseous infusion devices that revolutionised the ability to infuse blood on helicopters. In the four years after the introduction of the Massive Transfusion Protocol, 417 casualties required massive transfusion at Bastion. A higher proportion of casualties survived, without a change in injury severity, and the changes in military transfusion practice and capability contributed significantly to this.[127]

> These transfusion advances fulfilled Cohen's three criteria for determining revolution.

Damage control radiology

Andrew Krepinevich (1994) had incorporated *'the application of new technologies'* when defining revolution, p.9. This applies to battlefield radiology in the last decade. Until 2004, the standard UK operational radiology service was provided by radiographers, and involved mobile x-ray units, cumbersome wet film processing, and portable ultrasound machines, with no deployed radiologists. Radical changes came thereafter:

> 2004 – Direct digital radiography introduced at BMH Shaibah, Iraq
> 2005 – First CT scanner deployed to Shaibah
> 2007 – CT scanner installed at Bastion
> 2009 – First consultant radiologist deployment
> 2010 – Two upgraded fast CT scanners replaced original at Bastion
> 2011 – MRI scanner installed at Bastion

Direct digital radiography (also introduced in 2007 at Bastion) replaced wet film processing, and provided instantly accessible radiography images in the emergency department. This facilitated rapid decision making and initiation of immediate resuscitative measures.[128]

CT scanning materially influences decision making in trauma, which is why CT scanners are mandatory within civilian trauma centres. However, cost, bulky equipment and the logistics of scanning critically ill patients had previously precluded their deployment. Once sizable numbers of combat casualties began to be incurred in Iraq, organisational interests came to the fore.[129]

Once radiologists commenced deploying to Bastion in May 2009 they were incorporated into trauma teams (a novel departure from NHS practice), adding consultant-performed Focused Abdominal Sonography for Trauma (FAST) and near-instantaneous reporting of CT scans to trauma resuscitation.[130]

The two upgraded (64-slice) fast CT scanners installed at Bastion in July 2010 produced images with 10 times more detail, in only a fraction of the time, scanning from head to toe in 18 seconds. This initiated the era of 'damage control radiology',[131] and radically changed trauma practice and outcomes, with the 'tunnel of death' becoming the 'circle of life'.[132] A similar progression to deployment of radiologists and fast CT scanners occurred with US Forces in Iraq (Balad) and in Afghanistan (Kandahar).[133]

> These imaging advances fulfilled Cohen's three criteria for determining revolution.

---

127   *Ibid.*

128   Duffy, 2015, pp.43–48
129   O'Reilly & Kilbey, 2007, pp.165–167
130   Gay & Miles, 2011, pp.S289–292
131   *Ibid.*
132   Duffy, 2015, pp.43–48
133   Beckett, et al, 2012, pp.2072–2077

Personal protective equipment

Prevention is better than cure. Personal (and vehicular) protective equipment has improved markedly across NATO since 2001 in response to IED technology.[134] In the UK this is largely due to close collaboration between various powerhouses – the Academic Department of Military Emergency Medicine (ADMEM, whose staff attend all military post-mortems to deduce lessons from injury patterns), the Defence Science and Technology Laboratory at Porton Down, the Royal British Legion Centre for Blast Studies at Imperial College London, and Defence Clothing manufacturers.[135]

Defence radiologists have contributed uniquely to protective equipment. From 2007 they carried out post-mortem CT scanning in Bastion of all UK personnel who died from IED explosions. This has helped identify ways to prevent and mitigate otherwise fatal injury, as well as guide research into novel treatment strategies.[136]

High-quality protection to the head (the Kevlar Mark 7 helmet), eyes (ballistic 'cool-looking' Wiley-type eyewear), and torso (Osprey body armour) is now standard. The result has been a commensurate fall in injuries to vulnerable areas.[137] Even better equipment, the Virtus body armour system, will shortly come into service.[138]

Prosthetics and analgesia

'This remarkable decade of medical innovation has also seen outstanding developments in artificial limbs and other appliances…'

Brigadier Chris Parker, 2013.[139]

Two key examples of organisational interests enabling transformation are in prosthetics and battlefield analgesia.

The moral imperative to provide the best care possible for service personnel wounded on duty extended to their recovery, with the UK Government promising war amputees top-class prosthetics for the rest of their lives.[140] Funds were made available for prosthetic research and development, and the very highly motivated and fit young amputees (many double and some triple amputees) provided the ideal testing ground for novel prosthetic techniques and devices.[141]

Perhaps the most exciting recent innovation has been the development of osseo-integration, whereby a titanium rod is inserted into the bone, protrudes through the end of the stump, and allows the prosthesis to be rapidly and securely clicked on to it, making the prosthesis part of the skeletal structure.[142]

134   Gilbert, 2013, pp.1 – 8
135   Hodgetts, et al, 2007c, pp.252 – 254
136   Singleton, et al, 2013
137   Penn-Barwell, et al, 2015, pp.1014 – 1020
138   Muncey, 2015, pp.34 – 38

139   Parker, 2013, p.10
140   Hi-tech prosthetics are getting our injured back on their feet. *The Daily Telegraph*, 19 January 2010
141   Poulter, 2013, https://www.gov.uk/government/news/11-million-funding-boost-to-improve-nhs-care-for-war-veterans (5 August 2015).
142   Goldthorpe, 2015, pp.36 – 39

Amputations and other serious injuries are often accompanied by severe pain. The Surgeon General, Louis Lillywhite, included pain control in his 'Main Effort' during his tenure.[143] This empowered DMS clinicians, and effective measures for battlefield analgesia have now been introduced throughout the casualty's chain of care.[144,145]

Summary

This chapter has discussed many major technological innovations introduced throughout the military trauma system, and their dramatic results.

The next chapter will argue how the DMS has 'transformed in contact', learning from operational experience to adapt and innovate organisationally and operationally, particularly through the development of powerhouses along the chain of patient care, resulting in unprecedented survival rates and functional outcomes.

143   Lillywhite, 2009a, pp.244–245

144   Aldington, et al, 2011, pp.268–275

145   Buckenmaier, et al, 2012, pp.919–926

The chain of care (Casualty arrival at Camp Bastion) David Rowlands, artist. With permission

Chapter 3:
Organisational and Operational Revolution

Wars forge change, not always sequentially or immediately. Building on doctrinal developments and technological innovations, several other drivers have also forced organisational change in the DMS, improving patient safety and outcomes. This chapter will focus on the following drivers: clinical governance, data capture and analysis, operational feedback (leading to the new role of Deployed Medical Director), clinical outcomes, and multinational collaboration. It will then concentrate on the powerhouses that have resulted from organisational adaptation.

Embracing clinical governance

'Was there a negligent failure to keep abreast of the developing state of knowledge?'

The Honourable Mr Justice Owen, High Court of Justice, 2003.[146]

A major impetus that led to the DMS introducing clinical governance to ensure best practice was the 2003 Post Traumatic Stress Disorder (PTSD) Class Action, in which Mr Justice Owen, above, criticised the DMS for not ensuring policy was implemented in practice.[147]

In response to this and to new clinical quality initiatives, under the leadership of Surgeon General Ian Jenkins (2002–2006) the DMS introduced 'Clinical Governance' (in essence Quality Assurance) to underpin all aspects of the care of soldiers on military operations.[148]

This change did not succeed overnight: 'It was clear that with the changes from Operation HERRICK 5 to 6 all corporate knowledge gathered during previous deployment had been lost … all Clinical Governance had to be started again.'

Permanent Joint Headquarters (PJHQ) Clinical Governance Team, 2007.[149]

Clinical governance improved once regular processes and procedures were instituted in 2007 to carry on from one roulement to another. The prime method was the weekly Joint Theatre Clinical Case Conference, reinforced by regular PJHQ assurance visits.

In January 2008, the new Surgeon General, Louis Lillywhite, requested the Healthcare Commission to undertake an independent review of the quality of healthcare services provided by the DMS:

'The DMS is very small and it can be extremely difficult to keep up with best practice across the whole spectrum of medical care. An external regulator would help us to identify where we are failing to adopt best emerging practice.'[150]

---

146   PTSD Class Action, 2003
147   McGeorge, et al, 2006, pp.22–28

148   Lillywhite, 2009b, pp.20–28
149   Batham, 2011, pp.50–55
150   Healthcare Commission Report, 2009, p.4

Lillywhite had come fresh to the role after heading the Directorate of Medical Operational Capability,[151] where he had fully embraced the concept of clinical governance:

'I concluded that if there were skeletons, it was better to expose them early, and to be able to demonstrate that by initiating the review ourselves we were committed to providing quality care'.[152]

The high standard of clinical care resulting from this sustained commitment to clinical governance was such that the Healthcare Commission subsequently described the DMS trauma services as 'exemplary'.[153]

Capturing data – Joint Theatre Trauma Registry (JTTR)

'The military will only reassure its critics by publishing clinical results both good and bad. ADMEM have produced a robust data capture and governance structure that should allow the military to go on a publishing offensive rather than forever remaining on the back foot.'

Keith Porter, Honorary Clinical Professor of Traumatology, University of Birmingham.[154]

Lawrence Freedman has emphasised how high-quality information gathering, correctly and promptly interpreted, allied to high-quality decision making, lies at the heart of military revolution.[155] This section argues that the establishment of an effective information management system by the DMS has transformed clinical outcomes.

UK experience

Apart from a 1970s databank of Northern Ireland casualties, the DMS had no effective system-wide means to capture operational clinical data well into the 1990s. This situation only changed when the introduction of an effective trauma registry during the 1999 Kosovo campaign catalysed further development.[156,157]

By contrast, the DMS now maintains at least four electronic medical datasets: the Joint Theatre Trauma Registry (the most important, discussed below), the Complex Trauma Database, the Prosthetics Database and the Defence Patient Tracking System. The Ministry of Defence now publishes regular reports, for instance on amputees, based on these.[158,159]

151   Director General Medical Operational Capability Report, 2006
152   Lillywhite, 2009b, p.27
153   Healthcare Commission Report, 2009, pp.13–17
154   Porter, 2007, p.243

155   Freedman, 1998, pp.55–66
156   Hodgetts, et al, 2000a, pp.134–142
157   Hodgetts, et al, 2000b
158   Defence Statistics (Health), 2015
159   Dharm-Datta, et al, 2011, pp.1362–1367

The Joint Theatre Trauma Registry (JTTR)

The **JTTR**, established at RCDM in 2003, underpins and has transformed so much of current practice that it is crucial to understand its provenance. Its aim is to maintain and improve the standard of care of the seriously injured patient in real time, from the point of injury to discharge from treatment. Fundamentally, it is a quality assurance system designed to detect unexpected outcomes (such as unexpected survivors or deaths, complications, adverse events or emerging injury patterns).[160,161]

The JTTR draws on three independent databases:

- Major trauma audit for clinical effectiveness (**MACE**)
- Medical emergency response team (**MERT**), which records all patients treated by the MERT in Afghanistan since 2006
- Operational emergency department attendance register (**OpEDAR**). This database, commenced in 2003 on Op TELIC, records all patients attending the emergency department of deployed UK field hospitals in order to audit and improve activity.[162]

The **MACE** project was established by Timothy Hodgetts in 1997 at Frimley Park Hospital, to collect and analyse data on seriously injured trauma patients.[163] It was replicated at 22 Field Hospital in Kosovo in June 1999, allowing direct comparison of performance against Frimley Park's benchmark data. This marked the beginning of regular auditing of clinical operational data by the DMS.[164]

In order to capture trauma data from multiple field hospitals deploying on Op TELIC (2003), the Academic Department of Military Emergency Medicine established the **Joint Theatre Trauma Registry** at RCDM, subsuming the MACE database. JTTR has become a large, prospectively collected database of every UK military casualty since 2003 who is either killed on operations or is subject to a trauma call and treated by a deployed medical facility ashore or afloat. It therefore includes all seriously injured casualties from Iraq and Afghanistan. Since 2007 it has also included all injured UK service personnel repatriated for treatment in Birmingham.[165]

The JTTR has proven invaluable as a major source for combat injury research, as was envisaged by Keith Porter (p.28), for instance providing data for many of the articles quoted in this work.

US experience

In 2004, the US military established the Joint Theater Trauma System (JTTS) under the direction of Colonel Brian Eastridge,[166] to emulate the dramatic successes of civilian trauma systems (that had originated from military experience in Vietnam) and thereby improve current battlefield care. The JTTS was a collaborative effort between the three Surgeon Generals of the US military, the US Army Institute of Surgical Research (the Army's lead combat casualty care research laboratory), and the American College of Surgeons Committee on Trauma.[167]

160   Hodgetts, 2012a, p.53
161   Russell, et al, 2011, pp.177 – 178
162   Russell, et al, 2007, pp.244 – 251
163   Hodgetts, et al, 1998
164   Hodgetts, et al, 2000b

165   Russell, et al, 2011, pp.177 – 178
166   COL (Ret) Brian Eastridge http://www.militarysurgeons.org/distinguished-faculty/col-brian-eastridge/ (20 August 2015)
167   Eastridge, et al, 2006, pp.1366 – 1373

Within this new system of powerhouses, the Institute of Surgical Research established a Joint Theater Trauma Registry, similar to the UK'S JTTR.[168] The many beneficial outcomes included new combat trauma clinical practice guidelines, resulting in improved resuscitation practices, and a gratifying rise in survival rates.[169,170]

Operational feedback – Joint Theatre Clinical Case Conference (JTCCC)

Before 2007 the DMS had no systemic method to provide regular and timely clinical feedback to deployed field hospitals, or to connect clinicians with planners. The JTCCC was therefore established by Timothy Hodgetts in 2007, at Bastion Hospital.[171] It became a weekly multidisciplinary telephone conference to discuss the management of current casualties, linking RCDM (military and civilian clinicians), deployed field hospitals, the Defence Medical Rehabilitation Centre (Headley Court), RAF Brize Norton (co-ordinating aeromedical evacuation back to the UK), 2 Medical Brigade (the organisation that trains the next deploying field hospital), Inspector General's department (overseeing all DMS governance) and PJHQ (the strategic headquarters for overseas operations).[172]

The JTCCC enabled the DMS to track casualties flowing through the trauma system, to identify and correct sub-optimal performance, and to measure outcomes, to ensure best practice was being followed and that urgent clinical lessons were immediately applied. The advantage of frequent meetings involving both clinicians and planners was that, whenever a problem was identified, so was the solution.[173] The JTCCC remains active today, as casualties are repatriated from wherever British Forces are stationed overseas.

The Deployed Medical Director

'The military machine … is basically very simple and very easy to manage. But we should bear in mind … each part is composed of individuals, every one of whom retains his potential for friction …'

Clausewitz, On War, 1832.[174]

Clausewitz, above, highlights the challenges posed by interpersonal friction, which are magnified in a multinational environment, requiring strong leadership and communication skills to mitigate effectively. The development of the Deployed Medical Director (DMD) role within the military medical machine exemplifies the importance of these leadership skills and operational experience in promoting transformation.[175]

Until early 2009, the senior doctor in British field hospitals doubled up as Clinical Director. This led to situations where a surgeon or anaesthetist, despite acting as Clinical Director, would be fully occupied in theatre and unable to deal with other crises. This had not presented an issue in the short periods of clinical activity during Op GRANBY or the opening phase of

168   Baer, et al, 2009, pp.327 – 332
169   Eastridge, et al, 2009, pp.852 – 857
170   Palm, et al, 2012, pp.S459 – S464
171   Willdridge, et al, 2010, pp.79 – 83
172   Russell, et al, 2011, pp.171 – 191

173   *Ibid.*
174   Howard & Paret, 2008
175   Mahoney, et al, 2011, pp.S350 – S356

Op TELIC (2003), or in quieter campaigns in between. It was a different matter once the pace and complexity of clinical activity accelerated in Afghanistan, with the change from ballistic to blast injury, when the Taliban adapted by using IEDs with telling effect.[176]

By 2009, many developments in combat casualty care in Afghanistan had come together. The advances in pre-hospital medicine and damage control resuscitation, the rapid evacuation of large numbers of massively wounded personnel to and from Bastion Hospital, the multinational working environment, the inter-disciplinary challenges of clinical innovations, and the high-intensity workload with its clinical dilemmas and ethical issues, had created extremely challenging conditions. These were too complex for individual clinical directors who still had to care personally for critically ill casualties, especially if they were unfamiliar with new concepts and processes.

These conditions, and operational feedback, led to the novel concept of the DMD. This person, an experienced and respected clinician, would be formally appointed in a leadership role, without direct clinical responsibilities, working in a triumvirate alongside the commanding officer and senior nursing officer, with direct managerial responsibility for clinical activity across the hospital.

The first DMD deployment was in April 2009 on Op HERRICK 10, just in time for the frenetic clinical activity that ensued from Operation Panther's Claw that summer. The first two DMDs were the experienced professors in anaesthesia (Peter Mahoney) and emergency medicine (Timothy Hodgetts) from RCDM; thereafter a robust selection process was introduced together with structured pre-deployment training, two intensive hospital validation exercises (HOSPEX) at Strensall, and finally a week-long handover in theatre.[177]

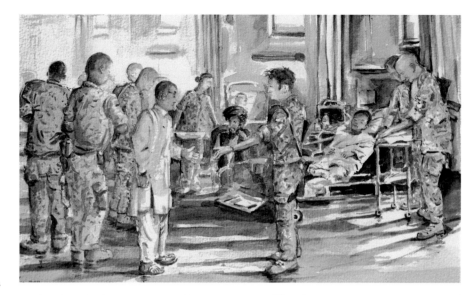

Deployed Medical Director on ward round at Bastion.[178]

DMDs have played a crucial co-ordinating role in meeting the complex challenges at Bastion, smoothing professional interactions, maintaining and developing high clinical standards, and addressing ethical dilemmas and challenges from one roulement of hospital staff to another. Moreover, they were the interface between the 'first world' facilities at Bastion and the various Afghan civilian, charitable and military medical facilities, as well as with other Allied hospitals in theatre.[179]

The success of the military medical trauma system owed much to the successive DMDs who deployed to Bastion, and proved the validity of the concept.

---

176   Johnson, 2013, pp.3 – 27
177   Mahoney, et al, 2011, pp.S350 – S356
178   Gora Pathak, orthopaedic surgeon and artist. With permission
179   Vassallo, 2015b, pp.160 – 166

The outcome – unexpected survivors

'The medical system was almost unbeatable. Without doubt I brought back over half a dozen of my soldiers who survived because of the medical professionalism that currently exists in Theatre...'

Lieutenant Colonel DSG Graham, Commanding Officer 2 Scots, 2011.[180]

Many service personnel and civilians owe their lives to the exemplary care they received during the short period of existence (2006 – 2014) of Bastion Hospital, and in the British field hospital in Basra, Iraq (2003 – 2009).

The most telling testament to this care is the number of **unexpected survivors**, those whose injuries were so life-threatening that they should have died (as judged by their injury severity scores and by subject matter experts).

Between April 2006 and July 2008, there were 75 unexpected survivors out of nearly 300 severe UK combat trauma cases.[181] This 25% ratio contrasted starkly with the best National Health Service ratio of 6%, and this remarkable ratio was maintained through later years.

By the end of 2011, Surgeon Vice-Admiral Philip Raffaelli, the Surgeon General, could report to the House of Commons that there had been some 210 unexpected survivors,[182] and by the end of 2012 the number of unexpected survivors had risen to 265.[183]

On this basis, I estimate that, by the end of conflict operations in 2014, there would have been some 300 unexpected survivors in all.

JTTR data also showed that the New Injury Severity Score associated with a 50% chance of survival rose annually from 32 in 2003 to 60 in 2012, with a score of 60 representing an expected death, and 75 representing un-survivable injury.[184] In other words, more casualties were surviving among those with the most severe wounds.

Perhaps the most startling finding, and the ultimate testimony to the improvement in care over the decade, was the revelation that 38 casualties survived with such severe injuries that the NHS classed them as 'unsurvivable'.[185]

Multinational collaboration

'The genesis for this book began as a conversation between medical officers and anesthesiologists from different coalition countries in a tent in Camp Bastion'

Combat Anesthesia: the first 24 hours (2015).[186]

---

180   Graham, 2011, p.4 – 2_1.
181   Russell, et al, 2011, pp.171 – 191
182   House of Commons Defence Committee, 2011, p.15, Q310
183   Penn-Barwell, et al, 2015, pp.1014 – 1020
184   *Ibid.*
185   Medical advances saw 38 troops live through 'un-survivable' injuries in Iraq and Afghanistan. *The Daily Telegraph*, 2 June 2015 http://www.telegraph.co.uk/news/uknews/defence/11646952/Medical-advances-saw-38-troops-live-through-un-survivable-injuries-in-Iraq-and-Afghanistan.html (14 June 2015)
186   Buckenmaier & Mahoney, 2015a, p.xxiii

This work has previously argued for the importance of collaboration between powerhouses. Four main areas of multinational medical collaboration have arisen from recent conflicts:

Shared trauma registries

The UK and US Joint Theatre Trauma Registries developed independently, in 2003 and 2004 respectively, but fundamentally they had a similarly structured approach to improving combat casualty care. This made it much easier, with mutual casualties in Bastion providing the incentive, for the Registries to be aligned with one another, allowing sharing of data and research.[187,188,189] This also facilitated the development of key performance indicators (evidence-based clinical practice guidelines) in both nations' trauma systems.[190]

Embedded multinational hospital personnel

Surgical teams from Estonia were embedded in Bastion from 2007, the Danish provided a field hospital squadron in 2009 and individual clinicians thereafter, and from May 2009 between 40 and 100 US personnel deployed to Bastion on six-month attachments.[191] In addition, British neurosurgeons and maxillofacial surgeons were embedded within the ISAF Hospital in Kandahar.[192] The overall success of this collaboration bodes well for future operations where multinational field hospitals will increasingly feature as military forces shrink in size and share their resources.

Shared best practice

This is exemplified by the recently published book *Combat Anesthesia: the first 24 hours*, quoted above. This major collaboration between the Uniformed Services University in the US and the RCDM in the UK, with 104 experts in different fields as co-authors, shares best practice for saving lives during the critical first day after injury.[193]

Multinational Working Groups

Following President Obama's state visit to the UK in May 2011, a high-level US-UK medical Task Force was set up to collaborate on combat casualty care, focusing on mental health and rehabilitation.[194]

Ultimately, this sharing of knowledge and best practice is directed towards a common goal: saving as many lives as possible.[195]

187   Morrison, et al, 2013a, pp.330 – 334
188   Brown, et al, 2010, pp.S116 – S122
189   Morrison, et al, 2013b, pp.218 – 225
190   Buckenmaier & Galloway, 2015, pp.275 – 282
191   Vassallo, 2015c, doi:10.1136/jramc-2015-000465
192   Eisenburg, et al, 2010, pp.1 – 6

193   Buckenmaier & Mahoney, 2015b
194   House of Commons Defence Committee, 2012
195   Gilbert, 2013

Multinational collaboration at Bastion.[196]

196   Graeme Lothian, artist. With permission

Powerhouses of revolution

This chapter will now examine the UK powerhouses that contributed to revolution, commencing with those that impacted most on training, as the successful outcome of so many survivors from complex war injury owes much to the high-calibre multidisciplinary and collective pre-deployment training of medical personnel.[197] This training improved significantly as the instructor cadre themselves deployed and learnt from their own experiences, confirming the importance of operational experience as a driver for transformation.

Preparing for war – BATLS, MOST and HOSPEX

The most significant developments in training have been in three specific areas: Battlefield Advanced Trauma Life Support (BATLS), Military Operational Support Training (MOST), and field hospital macrosimulation exercises (HOSPEX).

BATLS concentrated on individual skills, while MOST and HOSPEX training focused also upon non-technical skills (human factors), communication and teamwork, building upon individuals' own skills and competencies. The intent was to reduce to an absolute minimum the learning curve on arrival in theatre, to ensure patient safety from day one.

BATLS

This essential trauma course for all clinicians, discussed in Chapter 1, was thoroughly revised in 2005 and 2008 under the leadership of the Academic Professors at RCDM.[198,199] BATLS now takes account of doctrinal developments arising from the adoption of the paradigm <C>ABC, and covers four increasingly sophisticated levels of care: care under fire, tactical field care, field resuscitation and advanced resuscitation.

MOST

'Surgeons currently deployed in Afghanistan face the daily task of treating military personnel suffering severe, complex injuries from bomb blasts or gunshot wounds … MOST plays a very necessary part in ensuring that surgical teams about to deploy to Afghanistan are as prepared as possible for the work they are likely to be exposed to.'

John Black, President of the Royal College of Surgeons, England.[200]

The MOST Course delivers realistic trauma training to complete surgical teams at the Royal College of Surgeons in London, combining cadaveric dissections with advanced mannequin simulators. This premier simulation training course commenced in 2007 as an active collaboration between the Academic Department of Military Surgery and Trauma, RCDM, Joint Medical Command and the Royal College of Surgeons.[201] Clinicians returning from deployment instruct on each course, consolidating the training of those about to go to war.

---

197   Vassallo, 2015c, doi:10.1136/jramc-2015-000465

198   Hodgetts, et al, 2005
199   Hodgetts, et al, 2008
200   RCS News, 2010
201   Ramasamy, et al, 2010, pp.453 – 459

MOST ensures that each surgical team gains the necessary experience and competencies in the key tenets of damage control resuscitation and conflict surgery before facing battlefield trauma for real. It has revolutionised the ability of the military medical services to pass on individual and institutional memory, which had so often been lost after previous conflicts.

HOSPEX

'This facility has delivered continuity between Bastion Hospital staff, it has ensured that a patient is as safe on the first day of the new hospital team as he or she is on the last day of the old one ...'

Lieutenant Colonel Andy Griffiths, clinical director 2011 – 2014, Army Medical Services Training Centre (AMSTC), Strensall.[202]

Following experience on Op TELIC 1 (2003), it was recognised that there was a serious need to radically transform training for field hospitals to make them fit for role.[203] The result was the unique HOSPEX training programme, initiated that year, an exceptional instance of organisational adaptation in war. A life-size mock-up of a field hospital (reconfigurable for different theatres), the HOSPEX trainer, was set up in a warehouse at the AMSTC.

All deploying hospital staff (including attached overseas personnel) thereafter undertook two separate three-day periods of fully immersive simulation training in the HOSPEX trainer. HOSPEX training modelled casualty flows throughout the hospital and focused on non-technical skills (human factors)

and crew resource management, with emphasis on communication, situational awareness, leadership, followership and teamwork.

These assessment and validation training periods rigorously tested the organisational 'fitness for purpose' of Reserve and Regular field hospitals deploying abroad. They provided an unprecedented level of assurance for governance purposes, and were proven to improve performance on deployment.[204]

HOSPEX trainer at Strensall

The HOSPEX trainer has proven readily adaptable to other clinical scenarios, most notably the Ebola outbreak in West Africa. It was rapidly transformed in October 2014, effectively changing from being the best trauma hospital simulator in the world to the best Ebola treatment facility simulator in a few weeks.[205]

202   British Army website, http://www.army.mod.uk/news/26241.aspx (2 January 2015).
203   Cox & Roberts, 2008, pp.193 – 194

204   Arora, et al, 2014, pp.252 – 258
205   Vassallo, 2015c, doi:10.1136/jramc-2015-000465

Bastion Hospital

'For all of us here, especially medics, Afghanistan has been the defining operation of our military generation. It has been the catalyst which has catapulted us to the forefront of battlefield trauma care world-wide. This building, the Bastion Role 3 has been at the heart of that development.'

Lieutenant Colonel Jaish Mahan, final Commanding Officer Bastion Hospital.[206]

Theo Farrell emphasises the importance of sustained operational experience for transformation.[207] Bastion Hospital, as the only British hospital in Afghanistan (2006-2014), through which all medical personnel rotated on numerous occasions, was the catalytic powerhouse at the heart and front line of military medical transformation, and was for some years the busiest trauma hospital in the world.[208,209,210]

Many casualties owed their lives to the care they received during their 24 hours there,[211] not least the 27 servicemen documented in the remarkable photo-essay book by Caroline Froggatt.[212]

The layout of Bastion Hospital was purposely designed to facilitate trauma management. Its emergency department was immediately adjacent to the operating theatres (hence 'right turn resuscitation'), as well as to the blood bank, intensive therapy unit and CT scanners. This configuration was specifically praised as a model for NHS trauma services to emulate.[213]

The work done at Bastion Hospital was initially undertaken in parallel with the deployment in Iraq (Op TELIC, 2003-2009) (see Annex, p.60). Each of Britain's three Regular field hospitals deployed six times, and the 10 Reserve field hospitals deployed at least twice each, to Iraq and Afghanistan in 2001 – 2014, in addition to four Royal Navy and Royal Air Force hospital squadron deployments.[214]

This had the signal advantage of ensuring that all military medical staff rapidly developed operational experience, and felt ownership of responsibility for casualty care. Corporate knowledge was passed on and best practice was enhanced. The proof of this was the improved survival year-on-year of combat casualties.[215]

206   Mahan, 2014, p.231
207   Farrell, 2013a, p.3
208   Vassallo, 2015a, pp.79 – 83
209   Vassallo, 2015b, pp.160 – 166
210   Vassallo, 2015c, doi:10.1136/jramc-2015-000465
211   Buckenmaier & Mahoney, 2015b
212   Froggatt & Adams, 2013

213   National Audit Office, 2010
214   Vassallo, 2015a, pp.79 – 83
215   Penn-Barwell, et al, 2015, pp.1014 – 1020

Casualty arrival at Bastion.[216]

216   David Rowlands, artist. With permission

This rapid sharing of operational experience across the DMS, concentrated mainly through Bastion Hospital, across a sustained period longer than the First and Second World Wars combined, catalysed developments in working practices, equipment, training, doctrine and force protection. It resulted in an integrated and sophisticated trauma system that achieved national and international recognition as an exemplar for major trauma centres.[217]

Royal Centre for Defence Medicine

The main UK powerhouse since 2001 has been the RCDM at Birmingham, now a centre for both academic and clinical excellence, receiving all injured service personnel from overseas. Its genesis following the nadir of the DMS in the late 1990s proves the validity of Barry Posen's hypothesis in his seminal work on military innovation theory: an organisation facing defeat can be spurred to innovate.[218]

At the end of the Cold War (1990), there were 14 British military hospitals still in existence, and the three Services had their own separate centres of academia and clinical excellence.

Drastic restructuring occurred with the post-Cold War peace dividend cuts of the 1994 Defence Cost Studies.[219] DCS 15 (*Front Line First*) direly affected the medical services. It resulted in wholesale closure of military hospitals, with the sole survivor in the UK, the Royal Hospital Haslar, becoming tri-service. Military clinicians were dispersed into five small Ministry of Defence Hospital Units (MDHUs) within NHS hospitals. Unsurprisingly, many experienced personnel left and there was a huge drop in morale and corporate knowledge.

By 1997, the House of Commons Defence Committee questioned whether the DMS could even continue to exist, and concluded that it would be unable to respond to the demands of a new conflict.[220] Faced with this existential challenge, the DMS innovated, under the leadership of the remaining cadre of hospital consultants.[221] It was decided to partner military healthcare even closer with the NHS, to close Haslar, and to open a centre of academic military medicine at a leading university hospital – this becoming the RCDM in Birmingham.[222]

The RCDM officially opened on 2 April 2001 at Selly Oak NHS Trust Hospital. The initial problems encountered when injured servicemen began returning from conflict in Iraq and Afghanistan to a NHS without experience in dealing with war wounds were surmounted under the leadership of Colonel Chris Parker, appointed Commandant 2006 – 2009, and the main civilian lead, Professor Keith Porter.[223]

In June 2010 RCDM and Selly Oak Hospital relocated to the new Queen Elizabeth Hospital Birmingham. Injured service personnel would there be treated in a dedicated 32-bed trauma and orthopaedic ward within a military environment.[224,225] The Queen Elizabeth Hospital and the RCDM have become the leading trauma hospital in the UK, and this strong civilian-military partnership is a role model for co-operation, co-ordination and achievement.[226] The care casualties received at RCDM prepared them well for rehabilitation at the next powerhouse on their road to recovery, the Defence Medical Rehabilitation Centre at Headley Court.

217   National Audit Office, 2010
218   Posen, 1984, p.47
219   Raffaelli, 2011, p.123

220   House of Commons Defence Committee, 1999
221   Lillywhite, 2009a, pp.244 – 245
222   Jenkins, 2004, pp.153 – 158
223   Parker, 2013, pp.10 – 11
224   Evriviades, et al, 2011, pp.219 – 230
225   Hollingsworth, 2012, pp.21 – 25
226   Porter, 2012, pp.22-24

Headley Court and rehabilitation

'They have served their country, buried their mates, cheated death itself and now rise above the hurt their enemies thought they had inflicted on them.'

General the Lord Dannatt, Chief of the General Staff 2006–2009.[227]

General the Lord Dannatt was here paying testimony to wounded service personnel who had journeyed to recovery through the Defence Medical Rehabilitation Centre (DMRC) at Headley Court, Surrey. Headley Court was established in 1946 in the aftermath of the Second World War, but re-entered the nation's consciousness at the beginning of the 21st century largely through the fund-raising activities of the charity, Help for Heroes.

Casualties entered Headley once they left the acute care environment of RCDM, in order to mobilise and return to fitness and work as far as possible. Headley had been transformed completely during the Iraq and Afghanistan conflicts in response to receiving large numbers of complex polytrauma casualties. In 2006, Headley had four beds and no staff, and 26 patients throughout the year; the following year, there were 10 times the number, even before the casualty surges in Afghanistan of 2009–2010.

That was only the beginning and smallest part of the challenge to innovate:

'Trying to mobilise somebody with no legs is tricky. To mobilise someone with a fractured pelvis and no legs is even trickier'.

Colonel John Etherington, Director, DMRC.[228]

Between 2003 and 2014, in Afghanistan alone, 265 British servicemen sustained 416 amputations – all who survived would eventually go through Headley.[229] Many would be admitted intermittently over four years or more, also undergoing maybe 25–40 operations, their complex multidisciplinary care being closely co-ordinated with RCDM. Rehabilitation services simultaneously expanded at Birmingham and at smaller units elsewhere.

The number of new patients thankfully tailed off after Afghanistan, in the inevitable lull before the next conflict, while the aging Headley Court was replaced in 2018 by a purpose-built state-of-the-art Defence and National Rehabilitation Centre, at Stanford Hall near Loughborough, for rehabilitation work continues – often in association with the next powerhouse, dealing with the mental trauma of injury.

227   Dannatt, 2013, p.13

228   Etherington, 2014. http://www.gresham.ac.uk/lectures-and-events/the-work-of-the-defence-medical-rehabilitation-centre-headley-court (3 August 2015)

229   Edwards, et al, 2015, pp.2848–2855

King's College and mental health

Psychiatric battle casualties feature significantly in modern warfare. The equivalent paradigm shift to the <C>ABC concept for physically wounded casualties was the formal recognition of 'Post Traumatic Stress Disorder' (PTSD) as a distinct entity in 1980.[230]

This chapter examines how the Ministry of Defence responded to the challenge of mitigating the psychological effects of sending military personnel into danger through the novel engagement of a civilian-military powerhouse, and two preventive strategies.

The First and Second World Wars showed that the number of psychiatric casualties is related to combat intensity and that effective clinical interventions can be applied.[231] However, prior to Op TELIC (2003), the British military had no mechanism to measure the mental health of their personnel. Two factors then brought about a radical change to this situation.

Firstly, this impending second war in Iraq awakened concerns of a repeat of the costly 'Gulf War Syndrome' saga of the 1990s, when many military personnel eventually developed unexplainable poor physical health. The MoD was accused of being slow to react to concerns and could not respond adequately due to poor record keeping. [232]

Secondly, the MoD was again caught on the back foot when criticised in the 2003 PTSD Class Action for potential negligence to keep abreast of modern knowledge [on battleshock] or to ensure practice followed doctrine.[233]

These criticisms made the MoD realise that, besides caring for wounded or ill service personnel, it had to carry out robust mental health surveillance.

The King's Centre for Military Health Research (KCMHR, led by Professors Simon Wessely and Edgar Jones) at King's College London, which had carried out research into 'Gulf War Syndrome',[234] was therefore commissioned to proactively monitor the health impact of Op TELIC. This was in collaboration with RCDM's Academic Centre for Defence Mental Health (led by Surgeon Commander Neil Greenberg).[235,236]

This ongoing programme, expanded to cover conflict in Afghanistan, has shown that generally the mental health of deployed British personnel remains good, though reservists and medics, and those exposed to violent conflict, fare slightly worse. Alcohol misuse and depression have proven more significant a problem than PTSD.[237]

The two preventive mental health strategies introduced over the last decade are Decompression and Trauma Risk Management.[238]

Decompression

Whereas servicemen returning from the Falklands war had time to adjust while travelling by sea, in the early days of conflict in Iraq and Afghanistan servicemen could be in peril in the morning and have flown home by evening. Individual augmentees or reservists returning on their own rather than with formed units, in particular, did not cope well with this sudden change.

230   Jones & Wessely, 2007, pp.164–175
231   Jones & Wessely, 2001, pp.242–247
232   Wessely, 2013, pp.201–212
233   PTSD Class Action, 2003, paragraph 5.116

234   Greenberg & Wessely, 2008, e10
235   Greenberg, et al, 2011, pp.261–267
236   KCMHR and ADMMH publications http://www.kcl.ac.uk/kcmhr/pubdb (7 July 2015)
237   MacManus, et al, 2014, pp.125–130
238   Greenberg, et al, 2011, pp.261–267

The British military therefore instituted a system of 'third location decompression' to smooth this transition, enforcing a short stopover in Cyprus en route to give troops opportunity to swim, sail and relax before finally heading home.

Research by KCMHR showed that troops generally thought decompression had been useful, and that it had a positive impact upon alcohol use and mental health for soldiers with a low to moderate degree of combat exposure.[239]

Trauma Risk Management

In the late 1990s, the Royal Marines developed a system of peer-provided psychological first aid called Trauma Risk Management (TRiM). TRiM was formally adopted as best practice throughout the Armed Forces in 2007.[240]

TRiM is delivered by unit personnel, not by health professionals. It emphasises the normality of emotional reactions to trauma, thereby avoiding medicalising distress. While not designed to prevent or treat PTSD, it positively changes attitudes to mental health, countering its stigma, and certainly appears to be beneficial, both for individuals and the unit.[241,242]

Imperial College and Blast Injury Studies

One of the most significant powerhouses to arise from recent conflict is the active collaboration of one of the world's leading research establishments (Imperial College London) with the RCDM in Birmingham, sponsored by the Royal British Legion, to create the Royal British Legion Centre for Blast Injury Studies (CBIS).[243]

The CBIS is the first collaboration of its kind in the UK, where civilian engineers and scientists work alongside military doctors, supported by charitable funding, to reduce the effects of IEDs – the leading cause of death and injury on recent operations. The interdisciplinary approach of this Centre, which only opened on 7 December 2011, is already radically transforming blast injury research and mitigation.[244]

Summary

The powerhouses discussed in this chapter are remarkable examples of organisational adaptation to meet new operational challenges. It would be difficult to overestimate the impact they have had on battlefield trauma care. They have not only revolutionised combat casualty care, they also have a particularly important role in continuing research and training post-conflict. The next chapter will discuss how revolution is sustained in between conflict.

239   Jones, et al, 2013, doi:10.1136/oemed-2012-101229
240   Greenberg, et al, 2008, pp.124 – 127
241   Greenberg, et al, 2010, pp.430 – 436
242   Wessely, 2013, pp.201 – 212

243   Centre for Blast Injury Studies http://www.imperial.ac.uk/blast-injury (28 June 2015)
244   CBIS Annual Report 2014, 2015

Chapter 4:
Sustaining Revolution

For military medical revolution to succeed, key lessons must be transferrable into civilian practice, for that is where military clinicians work and stay current in peacetime. These lessons also need to be embedded in doctrine, training and lessons learned processes, to ensure they are remembered for the next conflict.

Civilian adoption of military innovation

'Lessons from war must be remembered'

Professor Sir Bruce Keogh KBE, NHS Medical Director, and
Professor Keith Willett, first National Clinical Director for Trauma, 2012.[245]

'There are various reasons why the principles and procedures evolved in World War II concerning the treatment of the wounded are not yet an adequate part of medical practice. When it comes to transmitting experience in a positive way, a curious but understandable human inertia appears ...'

Henry Beecher, 1951.[246]

Beecher's comment on inertia is as relevant today, which may explain why some lessons need re-learning with each conflict, and why strong leadership is required if lessons are to transfer successfully to civilian practice.

The whole-hearted commitment by the leaders of the NHS, above, to ensure that modern UK trauma practice does take on board lessons from conflict is encouraging. The UK military has developed an exemplary trauma system – the NHS can only gain from assigning as much importance to the systemic management of major trauma as has the military.[247,248]

One promising example is in rehabilitation. In 2013, Headley Court's Director, John Etherington, was appointed National Clinical Director for Rehabilitation and Recovering in the Community for the NHS England, specifically to enhance NHS rehabilitation and prosthetic services by emulating the lessons and practices of Headley.[249]

In the Western world, there has been tremendous synergy over the last decade, as key lessons and practices are subsumed into trauma centres and national trauma systems by clinicians (reservists and regulars) returning from the battlefields.[250,251,252,253,254,255,256]

---

245   Keogh & Willett, 2012, pp.3 – 4
246   Beecher, 1951, pp.193 – 200

247   Hodgetts, et al, 2007d, pp.237 – 238
248   House of Commons Defence Committee, 2012
249   Etherington, 2014. http://www.gresham.ac.uk/lectures-and-events/the-work-of-the-defence-medical-rehabilitation-centre-headley-court (3 August 2015)
250   Holcomb, et al, 2007, pp.307 – 310
251   Davies & Thomas, 2009, pp.527 – 535
252   Tai, 2009a, pp.246 – 247
253   Brisebois, et al, 2011, pp.S124–S129
254   McCullough, et al, 2014, pp.202 – 206
255   Bogert, et al, 2014, doi: 10.1177/0885066614558018
256   Howell, 2014, pp.201 – 202

Some key lessons transferring into civilian practice are: leadership and delivery of care by consultant-led multidisciplinary trauma teams, strong orientation towards damage control resuscitation (including infrastructure design, with CT scanners and operating theatres immediately adjacent to emergency departments), major trauma and massive transfusion protocols, team and simulation training, robust clinical governance, real-time information management, and improved rehabilitation.[257,258]

Moreover, many of these lessons and innovative technologies (e.g. tourniquets) are simple and low cost – the paradigm <C>ABC itself costs nothing – and eminently suitable for low-income countries, where the bulk of trauma worldwide is sustained.[259] Overcoming that 'curious but understandable human inertia' to ensure these lessons reach round the earth is the challenge for global trauma care.

Promoting military medical research

Education and research promote and sustain best practice. The last 15 years of conflict have seen an outpouring of military medical research, with many influential articles and military-themed supplements appearing in leading world journals.[260,261,262,263] At least one major UK-US collaborative book has been published,[264] and other books document lessons from conflict.[265,266]

There has been a sea change in the encouragement given to UK military clinicians (including nurses, allied health professionals and medical support officers) to undertake research since 1990. Nowadays all UK military medical trainees and many consultants take postgraduate degrees, many up to doctoral level, a much higher proportion than among their NHS counterparts (Defence Deanery, personal communication). The Academic Department of Military Surgery and Trauma (at RCDM) has also established working groups to promote best practice and act as a focus for research.[267,268]

Several powerful UK academic powerhouses have been established (listed below) with significant effects.[269,270,271,272]

2001 – Royal Centre for Defence Medicine
2003 – King's Centre for Mental Health Research
2008 – Academic Department of Military Anaesthesia and Critical Care
2010 – MSc Trauma Surgery (Military)
2011 – Royal British Legion Centre for Blast Injury Studies
2012 – Association of Trauma and Military Surgery.

257 National Audit Office, 2010
258 Lamb, et al, 2014, pp.242 – 249
259 Chatfield-Ball, et al, 2015, pp.93 – 100
260 Orman, et al, 2012, pp.S403 – S408
261 Glassberg, et al, 2014, pp.126 – 131
262 Balazs, et al, 2015, pp.2777 – 2784
263 JRAMC website http://jramc.bmj.com (20 August 2015). Replaced by BMJ Military Health as of February 2020. https://militaryhealth.bmj.com
264 Buckenmaier & Mahoney, 2015b
265 Nessen, et al, 2008
266 Savitsky & Eastridge, 2012

267 Clasper, et al, 2007, pp.172 – 174
268 Brown, et al, 2012, pp.536 – 543
269 Military Anaesthesia, http://www.niaa.org.uk/Military-Anaesthesia (29 June 2015)
270 Swansea University, 2010, http://www.swansea.ac.uk/postgraduate/taught/medicine/msc-trauma-surgery-military/#key-features=is-expanded (10 July 2015)
271 CBIS, 2015, Annual Report 2014
272 ATMS Newsletter, 2012

Transforming after conflict

Post-Afghanistan, as after every major conflict, the major challenge is to ensure that lessons learned in developing an effective and integrated military trauma care system are not forgotten before the next conflict. The best and most enduring way to do this is to embed lessons into doctrine and training, and to ensure research continues.

Training and research require sustained funding and commitment, sometimes difficult to ensure between conflicts (when militaries are under political pressure to cut costs, as happened in the mid-1990s). This is where the powerhouses discussed previously have a particularly important role in sustaining momentum.

BATLS, MOST and HOSPEX, the most significant training processes, reflect current doctrinal concepts. It will be vital to ensure that training remains current and adaptable to meet developing threats.

The DMS has taken lessons learned processes to heart.[273,274] The US military medical services and the US Defense Health Board have similarly developed strategies to preserve recent combat trauma lessons for the future.[275]

'What matters most'. Casualty care during Ebola epidemic, 2015. Stuart Brown, artist. With permission

273   Brown, et al, 2012, pp.536 – 543
274   Defence Medical Services, https://www.gov.uk/government/groups/defence-medical-services# director-medical-policy-and-operational-capability (20 August 2015)
275   Defense Health Board, 2015

Conclusion

'Medical presence available to combatants of 2015 will be significantly different from that experienced by combatants in conflicts as recent as the 1990–91 war against Iraq.'

Colonel Scott Beaty, The Revolution in Military Medical Affairs, 1997.[276]

Scott Beaty, above, Director of the US Army Center for Healthcare Education and Studies, was the first to coin the phrase 'Revolution in Military Medical Affairs', predicting a *potential* medical revolution due to the changed geostrategic environment after the Cold War.

Cohen's three tests (modified by Hodgetts), pp.9–11, determine whether a military medical revolution has occurred: do military [medical] forces look fundamentally different, are the processes different, and are [clinical] outcomes also different?

This work has argued that Cohen's three tests have been met comprehensively by the Defence Medical Services, across the whole range of practice, with sufficient evidence provided to indicate the same applies for the US and other NATO Allies. The DMS now is fundamentally different to how it looked and functioned in 1990, some key examples being simulation training, consultant-led multidisciplinary trauma teams, damage control resuscitation, massive transfusion protocols, information management, clinical governance, and improved rehabilitation. Clinical outcomes have been transformed.

This is exemplified by perhaps the most iconic image of recent years (cover): that of the consultant-led MERT evacuating a critically wounded soldier from the battlefield, a soldier who would become an unexpected survivor. This would have been unthinkable in the Cold War.

Intense operational experience has galvanised the military medical services. The conceptual <C>ABC paradigm shift has driven radical doctrinal, operational and organisational changes, allied with significant technological innovations. This has led to superlative overarching military trauma systems [Cohen's 'processes']. Marshall, Krepinevich and Gray's criteria for a revolution in military affairs (pp.9–10), adapted for a medical context, have been fulfilled.

The most crucial feature of the organisational adaptations is the different powerhouses that have arisen under the leadership of dedicated individuals, in training through to rehabilitation, and that, as Heidi Doughty said (p.7), have resulted in 'a revolution in the continuity of care, based on collaboration'. These are vital to preserve the lessons of war.

Clausewitz defined war, fundamentally, as a 'clash of wills'. General the Lord Dannatt praised unexpected survivors for rising 'above the hurt their enemies thought they had inflicted on them' (p.40). The enemy seeks to hurt, we seek to heal. This is military medicine at its Clausewitzian core. It is by success in pursuing clinical outcomes that one judges whether a revolution in military medical affairs has occurred, but also whether we are winning this war, and by sustaining revolution whether we are placing ourselves to win the next.

---

276   Beaty, 1997–98, pp.60–72

There are some 300 unexpected UK survivors alone from the conflicts in Iraq and Afghanistan. This unprecedented survival rate [the clinical outcome] is due to the efforts of thousands of committed Service and multinational personnel who transformed the DMS into a world-class organisation barely 10 years after its nadir in the mid-1990s, and have sustained it since then.

Between Op GRANBY (1990) and Op GRITROCK (2015), the British military medical services successfully adapted and innovated organisationally and operationally from the Cold War paradigm (worst-case mass-casualty planning) to a new paradigm where the highest-calibre medical teams retrieve individual wounded soldiers, with unprecedented probability of survival and recovery. From quantity to quality. This transformation across the whole military trauma system has resulted in a radical change in the character and practice of military medicine, with spillover into global trauma care.[277]

In conclusion, the fulfilment of Cohen's tests shown by the evidence gathered herein shows conclusively how Beaty's prediction for military medicine in 2015 has come true. There has indeed been a Revolution in Military Medical Affairs.

Casualty evacuation in the Green Zone. David Rowlands, artist. With permission

---

277 Epilogue: An excellent UK example of continuing collaboration between military and civilian powerhouses, embedding lessons learned in conflict into nationwide civilian trauma care, is the jointly produced NHS England publication 'Clinical Guidelines for Major Incidents and Mass Casualty Events' (November 2018), https://www.england.nhs.uk/publication/clinical-guidelines-for-major-incidents-and-mass-casualty-events/

Declaration of interest

I have a personal involvement in the subject of this work. I have served in the British Army Medical Services since 1983, specifically as a consultant general surgeon since 1994.[278] I participated in field hospital exercises in the Cold War before experiencing war for real on Op GRANBY in 1990. Since then I have deployed repeatedly to conflict zones, to Bosnia and Kosovo (where I participated in the first stirrings of this revolution), Sierra Leone, Iraq and Afghanistan, where I saw revolution gather apace and mature. My patients and many others have benefited greatly from the changes discussed here.[279]

The military medical system now is different from the one I joined in 1983, just as it will doubtless look different again in another 30 years' time, though the ethos remains the same: caring for the wounded in war.

---

278 Epilogue: I retired from active duty in 2018, three years after being awarded the MA (History of Warfare) by King's College London, and after 34 years' fulfilling service in Her Majesty's Armed Forces. Nonetheless, I remain actively involved in pre-deployment training, having developed a classroom-based HOSPEX Tabletop field hospital simulation exercise for training civilian and military field hospital staff. I also deliver 'Teach the Trainer' HOSPEX Tabletop sessions, to ensure that the lessons learned during this military medical revolution are passed on to those who serve and to those who care for conflict and disaster victims.

279 Epilogue: Many of the life-saving advances in military medicine highlighted in this work have subsequently been examined in detail in the multi-author 'Military Medicine in Iraq and Afghanistan – A Comprehensive Review' (Editor: Ian Greaves; CRC Press, 2019). My own contribution to this book was to write the two introductory chapters 'A brief history of Operations Telic and Herrick' and 'Organisation of the medical services in Iraq and Afghanistan', together with three annexes on the Forces and medical units deployed on both Operations.

The author, in desert combats, 2011

Bibliography

References are grouped under journal publications, books, PhD dissertation, reports and directives, newspaper articles, and websites.

Journal publications

Aldington, D. J., McQuay, H. J., & Moore, R. A. (2011).
End-to-end military pain management. *Phil. Trans. R. Soc. B*, 366:268-275.

Apodaca, A., Olson, C., Bailey, J., Butler, F., Eastridge, B., & Kuncir, E. (2013).
Performance improvement evaluation of forward aeromedical evacuation platforms
in Operation Enduring Freedom. *J Trauma Acute Care Surg*, 75 (2), Suppl 2:S157-S163.

Arora, S., Cox, C., Davies, S., Kassab, E., Mahoney, P., Sharma, E., et al. (2014).
Towards the next frontier for simulation-based training: full-hospital simulation
across the entire patient pathway. *Annals Surgery*, 260:252-258.

ATMS Newsletter. (2012).
The birth of a new surgical specialty association. *J Association of Surgeons of Great Britain
& Ireland*, September; (37):42 http://www.asgbi.org.uk/en/publications/Journals.cfm.

Baer, D. G., Dubick, M. A., Wenke, J. C., Brown, K. V., McGhee, L. L., Convertino, V. A., et al. (2009).
Combat Casualty Care Research at the U.S. Army Institute of Surgical Research.
J R Army Med Corps, 155 (4):327-332.

Bailey, M. S., Beaton, K., Bowley, D., Eardley, W., Hunt, P., Johnson, S., et al. (2015).
Bending the curve: force health protection during the insertion phase of the Ebola outbreak
response. *J R Army Med Corps*, 2016;162:191-197 (published online ahead of print)
doi:10.1136/jramc-2014-000375 (accessed 12 July 2015).

Balazs, G. C., Dickens, J. F., Brelin, A. M., Wolfe, J. A., Rue, J.-P. H., & Potter, B. K. (2015).
Analysis of Orthopaedic Research Produced During the Wars in Iraq and Afghanistan.
Clin Orthop Relat Res, 473:2777–2784 (published online ahead of print) doi:10.1007/s11999-
015-4244-7.

Batham, D. R. (2011).
Clinical Governance on Operation HERRICK 9 – a personal perspective.
J R Naval Med Service, 97 (2):50-55.

Beaty, S. (1997–98).
The Revolution in Military Medical Affairs. *Parameters*, 60-72.

Beckett, A., Pelletier, P., & Mamczak, C. (2012).
Multidisciplinary trauma team care in Kandahar, Afghanistan: Current injury patterns
and care practices. *Injury, Int. J. Care Injured*, 43:2072-2077.

Beckett, A., Callum, J., & Teodoro da Luz, L. (2015).
Fresh whole blood transfusion capability for Special Operations Forces.
Can J Surg, 58 (Issue 3 Suppl 3): S153 — S156.

Beecher, H., Simeone, F., Burnett, C., Shapiro, S., Sullivan, E., & Mallory, T. (1947).
The Internal State of the Severely Wounded Man on Entry to the Most Forward Hospital.
Surgery, 22:676.

Beecher, H. K. (1951).
Early Care of the Seriously Injured Man. *JAMA*, 145 (4):193-200.

Blackbourne, L. H., Baer, D. G., Eastridge, B. J., Kheirabadi, B., Kragh, J. F., Cap, A. P., et al. (2012a).
Military medical revolution: prehospital combat casualty care.
J Trauma Acute Care Surg, 73(6), Supplement 5, pp.S372 – S377.

Blackbourne, L. H., Baer, D. G., Eastridge, B. J., Renz, E. M., Chung, K. K., DuBose, J., et al. (2012b).
Military medical revolution: deployed hospital and en route care.
J Trauma Acute Care Surg, 73(6), Supplement 5, pp.S378 – S387.

Blackbourne, L. H., Baer, D. G., Eastridge, B. J., Butler, F. K., Wenke, J. C., Hale, R. G., et al. (2012c).
Military medical revolution: military trauma system.
J Trauma Acute Care Surg, 73(6), Supplement 5, pp.S388 – S394.

Bogert, J., Harvin, J., & Cotton, B. (2014).
Damage Control Resuscitation. *J Intensive Care Med.* 2016 Mar;31(3):177-86.
doi: 10.1177/0885066614558018. (published online ahead of print) (accessed 28 June 2015).

Boulton, F., & Roberts, D. J. (2014).
Blood transfusion at the time of the First World War – practice and promise at the birth of transfusion medicine. *Transfusion Medicine*, Dec;24(6):325-334. doi: 10.1111/tme.12171 http://onlinelibrary.wiley.com/doi/10.1111/tme.12171/pdf (accessed 28 June 2015).

Bricknell, M. (2014).
For debate: the Operational Patient Care Pathway. *J R Army Med Corps*, 160:164-169.

Brisebois, R., Hennecke, P., & Kao, R. (2011).
The Role 3 Multinational Medical Unit at Kandahar Airfield 2005–2010.
Can J Surg, Dec; 54(6 Suppl): S124–S129.

Brodie, S., Hodgetts, T., Ollerton, J., McLeod, J., Lambert, P., & Mahoney, P. (2007).
Tourniquet use in combat trauma: UK military experience.
J R Army Med Corps, 153 (4):310-313.

Brown, K. V., Dharm-Datta, S., Potter, B. K., Etherington, J., Mistlin, A., Hsu, J. R., et al. (2010). Comparison of development of heterotopic ossification in injured US and UK Armed Services personnel with combat-related amputations: preliminary findings and hypotheses regarding causality. *J Trauma*, 69 (Suppl 1):S116-S122.

Brown, K. V., Guthrie, H. C., Ramasamy, A., Kendrew, J. M., & Clasper, J. (2012).
Modern military surgery - lessons from Iraq and Afghanistan.
J Bone Joint Surg Br, 94-B:536–43.

Buckenmaier, C. T., Mahoney, P. F., Anton, T., Kwon, N., & Polomano, R. C. (2012).
Impact of an Acute Pain Service on pain outcomes with combat-injured soldiers at Camp Bastion, Afghanistan. *Pain Medicine*, 13:919-926.

Butler, F. K., Hagmann, J., & Butler, E. G. (1996).
Tactical combat casualty care in special operations. *Military Medicine*, 161(Suppl): 3–16.

Butler, F. K., Holcomb, J. B., Giebner, S. D., McSwain, N. E., & Baqian, J. (2007).
Tactical combat casualty care 2007: evolving concepts and battlefield experience.
Military Medicine, 172 (11 Suppl):1-19.

Butler, F. K., & Blackbourne, L. H. (2012).
Battlefield trauma care then and now: A decade of Tactical Combat Casualty Care.
J Trauma Acute Care Surg, 73(6), Supplement 5:S395-S402.

Carmont, M. R. (2005).
The Advanced Trauma Life Support course: a history of its development and review of related literature. *Postgrad Med J*, 81:87–91. doi: 10.1136/pgmj.2004.021543.

Chatfield-Ball, C., Boyle, P., Autier, P., Herzig van Wees, S., & Sullivan, R. (2015).
Lessons learned from the casualties of war: battlefield medicine and its implication for global trauma care. *J R Soc Med*, 108 (3): 93-100.

Clasper, J., Lower Limb Trauma Working Group. (2007).
Amputations of the lower limb: a multidisciplinary consensus. *J R Army Med Corps*, 153:172-174

Cohen, E. A. (2004).
Change and transformation in military affairs. *Journal of Strategic Studies*, 27 (3): 395-407.

Cox, C. F., & Roberts, P. (2008).
HOSPEX: A historical view and the need for change. *J R Army Med Corps*, 154:193-194.

Davies, R., & Thomas, G. O. (2009).
Battlefield resuscitation. *Current opinion in clinical care*, 15 (6):527-535.

Davies, R. L. (2015).
Should whole blood replace the shock pack?
J R Army Med Corps, 2016 Feb;162(1):5-7. doi:10.1136jramc-2015-000413 (published online ahead of print) (accessed 16 June 2015).

Davis, P. R., Rickards, A. C., & Ollerton, J. E. (2007).
Determining the composition and benefit of the pre-hospital Medical Response Team in the conflict setting. *J R Army Med Corps*, 153 (4):269-273.

Dharm-Datta, S., Etherington, J., Mistlin, A., Rees, J., & Clasper, J. (2011).
Outcome of amputees in relation to military Service. *Injury, Int. J. Care Injured*, 42:1362-1367.

Doughty, H., Woolley, T., & Thomas, G. (2011).
Massive Transfusion. *J R Army Med Corps*, 157(3 Suppl 1): S277-S283.

Duffy, P. (2015).
Battlefield Radiology: 2014 Update. *Journal of Military and Veterans' Health*, 23 (2): 43-48.

Eastridge, B. J., Jenkins, D., Flaherty, S., Schiller, H., & Holcomb, J. B. (2006).
Trauma System Development in a Theater of War: Experiences From Operation Iraqi Freedom and Operation Enduring Freedom. *J Trauma*, 61:1366 –1373.

Eastridge, B. J., Costanzo, G., Jenkins, D., Spott, M. A., Wade, C., Greydanus, D., et al. (2009). Impact of Joint Theater trauma system initiatives on battlefield injury outcomes. *American Journal of Surgery*, 198 (6):852-857.

Edwards, D. S., Phillip, R. D., Bosanquet, N., Bull, A. J., & Clasper, J. C. (2015). What Is the Magnitude and Long-term Economic Cost of Care of the British Military Afghanistan Amputee Cohort? *Clin Orthop Relat Res*, 473:2848–2855 (doi: 10.1007/s11999-015-4250-9 published online 1 June 2015).

Eisenburg, M. F., Christie, M., & Mathew, P. (2010). Battlefield neurosurgical care in the current conflict in southern Afghanistan. *Neurosurg Focus*, 28 (5):1-6.

Evriviades, D., Jeffery, S., Cubison, T., Lawton, G., Gill, M., & Mortiboy, D. (2011). Shaping the military wound: issues surrounding the reconstruction of injured servicemen at the Royal Centre for Defence Medicine. *Phil. Trans. R. Soc. B*, 366:219-230.

Freedman, L. (1998). Britain and the Revolution in Military Affairs. *Defense & Security Analysis*, 14 (1):55-66.

Gay, D., & Miles, R. M. (2011). Damage control radiology: an evolution in trauma imaging. *J R Army Med Corps, 157*((3 Suppl 1)), 157 (3) Suppl 1:S289–292 (Article also named 'Use of imaging in trauma decision-making').

Glassberg, E., Nadler, R., Erlich, T., Klien, Y., Kriess, Y., & Kluger, Y. (2014). A Decade of Advances in Military Trauma Care. *Scandinavian J Surg*, 103:126-131.

Goldthorpe, S. (2015, August). In feet first – Interview with Shaun Stocker. *Soldier Magazine*, pp.71:36 – 39 See also www.shaunstocker.co.uk (accessed 3 August 2015).

Gray, C. S. (2006, February). Recognizing and understanding revolutionary change in warfare: the sovereignty of context. *Strategic Studies Institute*, vi.

Greenberg, N., & Wessely, S. (2008). Gulf War syndrome: an emerging threat or a piece of history? *Emerging Health Threats Journal*, 1, e10. (doi:10.3134/ehtj.08.010) (accessed 3 August 2015).

Greenberg, N., Langston, V., & Jones, N. (2008). Trauma Risk Management (TRiM) in the UK armed forces. *J R Army Med Corps*, 154:124-127.

Greenberg, N., Langston, V., Everitt, B., Iversen, A., Fear, N. T., Jones, N., et al. (2010). A cluster randomized controlled trial to determine the efficacy of TRiM (Trauma Risk Management) in a military population. *J Trauma Stress*, 23:430-436.

Greenberg, N., Jones, E., Jones, N., Fear, N. T., & Wessely, S. (2011). The injured mind in the UK Armed Forces. *Phil. Trans. R. Soc. B*, 366:261-267.

Hamblen, D. L. (2012). Further opinion - Modern military surgery. *J Bone Joint Surg [Br]*, 94-B:536-43 doi:10.1302/0301-620X.94B4.29714.

Hess, J. R., Spinella, P., & Holcomb, J. (2008). Blood Use on the Battlefield: is Fresh Whole Blood making a comeback? *NHS Blood and Transplant*, (Autumn);26:9-10.

Hodgetts, T., Kenward, G., & Masud, S. (2000a). Lessons from the first operational deployment of emergency medicine. *J R Army Med Corps*, 146:134-142.

Hodgetts, T. J., Mahoney, P. F., Byers, M., & Russell, M. Q. (2006). ABC to <C>ABC: redefining the military trauma paradigm. *Emerg Med J*, 23, 745-746.

Hodgetts, T. J., & Mahoney, P. F. (2007a). The Military Tourniquet: a response. *J R Army Med Corps*, 153 (1):12-15.

Hodgetts, T., Mahoney, P., Kirkman, E., & Midwinter, M. (2007b). Damage Control Resuscitation. *J R Army Med Corps*, 153 (4):299-300.

Hodgetts, T., Davies, S., Midwinter, M., Russell, R., Smith, J., Clasper, J., et al. (2007c). Operational mortality of UK Service Personnel in Iraq and Afghanistan: a one year analysis 2006-7. *J R Army Med Corps*, 153 (4):252-254.

Hodgetts, T. J., Davies, S., Russell, R., & McLeod, J. (2007d). Benchmarking the UK military deployed trauma system. *J R Army Med Corps*, 153 (4):237-238.

Hodgetts, T. J., & Findlay, S. (2012b). Putting Role 1 First: The Role 1 Capability Review. *J R Army Med Corps*, 158(3):162-170.

Holcomb, J. B., Jenkins, D., & Rhee, P. (2007). Damage control resuscitation: directly addressing the early coagulopathy of trauma. *J Trauma*, 62:307-310.

Hollingsworth, A. C. (2012).
The Birmingham Military Trauma Registrar - A personal view.
J R Naval Medical Service, 98 (3):21-25.

Howell, S. J. (2014).
Advances in trauma care: a quiet revolution. *British Journal of Anaesthesia*, 113 (2):201-202.

Ingalls, N., Zonies, D., Bailey, J. A., Martin, K. D., Iddins, B. O., Carlton, P. K., et al. (2014).
Review of the First 10 Years of Critical Care Aeromedical Transport during Operation
Iraqi Freedom and Operation Enduring Freedom. *JAMA Surg*, 149 (8):807-813.

Jansen, J. O., Morrison, J. J., Midwinter, M. J., & Doughty, H. (2014).
Changes in blood transfusion practices in the UK role 3 medical treatment facility
in Afghanistan, 2008 – 2011. *Transfusion Medicine*, 24 (3):154-61.

Jenkins, I. (2004).
The changing world of military health care. *J R Naval Medical Service*, 90 (3):153-158.

Johnson, T. H. (2013).
Taliban adaptations and innovations. *Small Wars & Insurgencies*, 4 (1):3-27.

Jones, E., & Wessely, S. (2001).
Psychiatric battle casualties: an intra- and interwar comparison. *Br J Psychiatry*, 178:242-247.

Jones, E., & Wessely, S. (2007).
A paradigm shift in the conceptualization of psychological trauma in the 20th century.
Journal of Anxiety Disorders, 21:164-175.

Jones, N., Jones, M., Fear, N. T., Fertout, M., Wessely, S., & Greenberg, N. (2013).
Can mental health and readjustment be improved in UK military personnel
by a brief period of structured post-deployment rest (third location decompression)?
Occup Environ Med, Jul;70(7):439-45.

Keogh, B., & Willett, K. (2012).
Lessons from war must be remembered. *J R Naval Medical Service*, 98 (1):3-4.

Kozen, B. G., Kircher, S. J., Henao, J., Godinez, F. S., & Johnson, A. S. (2008).
An Alternative Hemostatic Dressing: Comparison of CELOX, HemCon, and QuikClot.
Acad Emerg Med, 15 (1):74-81.

Kragh, J. F., Dubick, M. A., Aden, J. K., McKeague, A. L., Rassmussen, T. E., Baer, D. G., et al. (2015).
U.S. Military use of tourniquets from 2001 to 2010. *Prehosp Emerg Care*, Apr – Jun;19 (2):184-90.

Kragh, J. F., Swan, K. G., Smith, D. C., Mabry, R. L., & Blackbourne, L. H. (2012).
Historical Review of Emergency Tourniquet Use to Stop Bleeding. *The American Journal of Surgery*, 203:242-252. http://dx.doi.org/10.1016/j.amjsurg.2011.01.028 (accessed 5 July 2015).

Kragh, J. F., Walters, T. J., Westmoreland, T., Miller, R. M., Mabry, R. L., Kotwal, R. S., et al. (2013).
Tragedy Into Drama: An American History of Tourniquet Use in the Current War.
J Special Operations Medicine, 13 (3):5-25.

Krepinevich, A. F. (1994).
Cavalry to Computer: The pattern of military revolution. *The National Interest*, (Fall):30-37.

Lamb, C., MacGoey, P., Navarro, A., & Brooks, A. (2014).
Damage control surgery in the era of damage control resuscitation.
British Journal of Anaesthesia, 113 (2): 242-249.

Lillywhite, L. (2009a).
The Past, Present and Future of the Defence Medical Services.
J R Army Med Corps, 155 (4):244-245.

Lillywhite, L. (2009b).
War and Medicine: The inter-relationship of war and medicine – lessons from current conflicts.
The RUSI Journal, 154 (5):20-28.

Lundberg, L., Molde, A., & Dalenius, E. (2008).
BATLS/BARTS/BBTLS Training for Swedish Armed Forces Medical Personnel
- A Ten Year Retrospective Study. *J Roy Army Med Corps*, 154 (1):34-37.

MacManus, D., Jones, N., Wessely, S., Fear, N. T., Jones, E., & Greenberg, N. (2014).
The mental health of the UK Armed Forces in the 21st century: resilience
in the face of adversity. *J R Army Med Corps*, 160:125-130.

Mahan, J. (2014).
Final address: closure of the Bastion Role 3 on 22 Sep 2014.
J R Naval Medical Service, 100 (3):231.

Mahoney, P.F. (2010).
Have you heard of MASH? *Bulletin Royal College of Anaesthetists*, 60:16-18.

Mahoney, P. F., Hodgetts, T. J., & Hicks, I. (2011).
The Deployed Medical Director: Managing the Challenges of a Complex Trauma System.
J R Army Med Corps, 157(3 Suppl 1): S350-S356.

Maughon, J. S. (1970).
An inquiry into the nature of wounds resulting in killed in action in Vietnam.
Military Medicine, 135:8-13.

McCullough, A. L., Haycock, J. C., Forward, D. P., & Moran, C. G. (2014).
Major trauma networks in England. *British Journal of Anaesthesia*, 113 (2):202-206.

McGeorge, T., Hacker Hughes, J., & Wessely, S. (2006).
The MoD PTSD decision: a psychiatric perspective. *Occupational Health Review*, 122:22-28.

Midwinter, M. (2009).
Damage control surgery in the era of damage control resuscitation.
J R Army Med Corps, 155 (4):323-326.

Morrison, J. J., Oh, J., DuBose, J., O'Reilly, D., Russell, R., Blackbourne, L., et al. (2013a).
En-route care capability from point of injury impacts mortality
after severe wartime injury. *Annals Surg*, 257:330-334.

Morrison, J. J., Ross, J. D., DuBose, J. J., Jansen, J. O., Midwinter, M. J., & Rassmussen, T. E. (2013b).
Association of cryoprecipitate and tranexamic acid with improved survival following
wartime injury: findings from the MATTERs II Study. *JAMA Surg*, 148 (3):218-225.

Muncey, S. (2015, July).
This time it's personal – the Army's new body armour system is about more than
just protection. *Soldier Magazine*, pp.34 – 38.

Nicholson Roberts, T., & Berry, R. (2012).
Pre-hospital trauma care and aero-medical transfer: a military perspective.
Contin Educ Anaesth Crit Care Pain , 12 (4):186-189.

O'Reilly, D. J., & Kilbey, J. (2007).
Analysis of the initial 100 scans from the first CT scanner deployed by the British
armed forces in a land environment. *J R Army Med Corps*, 153 (3):165-167.

Orman, J. A., Eastridge, B. J., Baer, D. G., Gerhardt, R. T., Rassmussen, T. E., & Blackbourne, L. H. (2012).
The impact of 10 years of war on combat casualty care research: a citation analysis.
J Trauma Acute Care Surg, 73 (6, Suppl 5): S403 – S408.

Palm, K., Apodaca, A., Spencer, D., Costanzo, G., Bailey, J., Blackbourne, L.H., Spott, M.A., Eastridge, B.J. (2012).
Evaluation of military trauma system practices related to damage-control resuscitation.
J Trauma Acute Care Surg, 73 (6), Suppl 5: S459-S464.

Parker, P., & Clasper, J. (2007).
The Military Tourniquet. *J R Army Med Corps*, 153 (1):10-12.

Parker, P., Nordmann, G., & Doughty, H. (2015).
Taking transfusion forward. *J R Army Med Corps*, 161 (1):2-4.

Patterson, C. M., Woodcock, T., Mollan, I. A., Nicol, E. A., & McLoughlin, D. C. (2014).
United Kingdom Military Aeromedical Evacuation in the Post-9/11 Era.
Aviation, Space, and Environmental Medicine, 85 (10):1005-1012.

Payne, M. (1995).
Appreciation - Brigadier Ian Haywood QHS.
Army Medical Services Magazine, 49 (February):71-72.

Penn-Barwell, J., Roberts, S. A., Midwinter, M. J., & Bishop, J. R. (2015).
Improved survival in UK combat casualties from Iraq and Afghanistan: 2003 – 2012.
J Trauma Acute Care Surg, 78 (5):1014-1020.

Porter, K. (2007).
Trauma governance in the UK Defence Medical Services – a commentary.
J R Army Med Corps, 153 (4):243.

Porter, K. (2012).
Care for the Courageous. *Surgeons News*, June:22 – 24 http://www.surgeonsnews.
com/back-issues and http://edition.pagesuite-professional.co.uk/Launch.
aspx?EID=10d3bfa3-2f03-4d31-894eca35a3ef9a77 (31 July 2015).

Raffaelli, P. (2011).
Preface – Military Medicine. *Phil Trans Soc B*, 366:123.

Ramasamy, A., Hinsley, D. E., Edwards, D. S., Stewart, M. M., & Midwinter, M. (2010).
Skill sets and competencies for the modern military surgeon: Lessons from UK military
operations in Southern Afghanistan. *Injury, Int. J. Care Injured*, 41:453-459.

RCS News. (2010).
Surgeons win military civilian partnership award, 26 November 2010. https://www.rcseng.
ac.uk/news/surgeons-win-military-civilian-partnershipaward (accessed 20 April 2015).

Rhee, P., Brown, C., Martin, M., Salim, A., Plurad, D., Green, D., et al. (2008).
QuikClot use in trauma for hemorrhage control: case series of 103 documented uses.
J Trauma, Apr;64(4):1093-1099.

Rice, D. H., Kotti, G., & Beninat, W. (2008).
Clinical review: Critical care transport and austere critical care. *Critical Care*, 12 (2):207.

Riley, B., & Mahoney, P. (1996).
Battlefield trauma life support: its use in the resuscitation department of 32 Field Hospital during the Gulf War. *Military Medicine*, 161(9):542-546.

Robertson, L. B. (1918).
A contribution on blood transfusion in war surgery. *Lancet*, 1:759-762.

Rosen, S.P. (2010). The Impact of the Office of Net Assessment on the American Military in the Matter of the Revolution in Military Affairs. *J Strategic Studies*, 33(4):469-482.

Russell, R. J., Hodgetts, T. J., Ollerton, J., Massetti, P., Skeet, J., Bray, I., et al. (2007).
The Operational Emergency Department Attendance Register (OpEDAR): a new epidemiological tool. *J R Army Med Corps*, 153:244-251.

Russell, R. J., Hodgetts, T. J., McLeod, J., Starkey, K., Mahoney, P., Harrison, K., et al. (2011). The role of trauma scoring in developing trauma clinical governance in the Defence Medical Services. *Phil. Trans. R. Soc. B*, 366:171-191.

Savage, E., Forestier, C., Withers, N., Tien, H., & Pannell, D. (2011).
Tactical Combat Casualty Care in the Canadian Forces: lessons learned from the Afghan war. *Can J Surg*, 54 (6 Suppl):S118–S123.

Singleton, J. A., Gibb, I. E., Hunt, N. C., Bull, A. M., & Clasper, J. C. (2013).
Identifying future 'unexpected' survivors: a retrospective cohort study of fatal injury patterns in victims of improvised explosive devices.
BMJ Open, 3:e003130. doi:10.1136/bmjopen-2013-003130.

Smith, E. R. (2014).
The Evolution of Civilian High Threat Medical Guidelines - How mass killing events have proven a need for new guidelines. *J Emergency Med Services*, (28 September) http://www.jems.com/articles/2014/09/evolution-civilian-high-threat-medical-g.html (28 May 2015).

Stoneham, J., Riley, B., Brooks, A., & Matthews, S. (2001).
Recent advances in trauma management. *Trauma*, 3:143-150.

Tai, N. (2009a).
Civilian Trauma Care and the Defence Medical Services - A Prospectus for Partnership? *J R Army Med Corps*, 155 (4):246-247.

Tai, N., Brooks, A., & Midwinter, M. (2009b).
Optimal Clinical Timelines - A Consensus from the Academic Department of Military Surgery and Trauma. *J R Army Med Corps*, 155 (4):253-256.

Tai, N. R., & Russell, R. (2011).
Right Turn Resuscitation: Frequently Asked Questions.
J R Army Med Corps, 157(3 Suppl 1): S310-S314.

Tarmey, N., Woolley, T., Jansen, J., Doran, C., Easby, D., Wood, P., et al. (2012).
Evolution of coagulopathy monitoring in military damage-control resuscitation.
J Trauma Acute Care Surg, 73(6), Supplement 5: S417-S422.

Turner, S., Ruth, M., & Tipping, R. (2009).
Critical Care Air Support Teams and deployed intensive care. *J R Army Med Corps*, 155(2): 171-174.

Vassallo, D. J., Sargeant, I. D., Sadler, P. J., & Barraclough, C. J. (1998).
Mass casualty incident at Hospital Squadron Sipovo, Bosnia following a Czech Hip helicopter crash, 8 Jan 1998. *J Roy Army Med Corps*, 144:61-66.

Vassallo, D. J., Klezl, Z., Sargeant, I. D., Cyprich, J., & Fousek, J. (1999).
British-Czech co-operation in a mass casualty incident, Sipovo. From aeromedical evacuation from Bosnia to discharge from Central Military Hospital, Prague. *J R Army Med Corps*, 145: 7-12.

Vassallo, D. J., Gerlinger, P., Maholtz, P., Burlingame, B., & Shepherd, A. F. (2003).
Combined UK/US Field Hospital Management of a Major Incident arising from a Chinook Helicopter Crash In Afghanistan, 28 Jan 2002. *J R Army Med Corps*, 149:47-52.

Vassallo, D. J., Graham, P., Gupta, G., & Alempijevic, D. (2005).
"Bomb Explosion On The Nis Express" – Lessons From A Major Incident, Kosovo 16 Feb 2001. *J R Army Med Corps*, 151:19-29.

Vassallo, D. (2014, Dec).
The Short Life and Times of Camp Bastion Hospital, Helmand, Afghanistan.
J ASGBI, 45, 16-21. http://www.publications.asgbi.org/jasgbi_12_12_14/jasgbi_winter2014.html#p=16.

Vassallo, D. (2015a).
A short history of Camp Bastion Hospital: the two hospitals and unit deployments.
J R Army Med Corps, 161 (1):79-83.

Vassallo, D. (2015b).
A short history of Camp Bastion Hospital: part 2 – Bastion's catalytic role in advancing combat casualty care. *J R Army Med Corps*, 161 (2):160-166.

Vassallo, D. (2015c).
A short history of Camp Bastion Hospital: preparing for war, national recognition and Bastion's legacy. *J R Army Med Corps*, 161(4);355-360 (published online June 2015 ahead of print). doi:10.1136/jramc-2015-000465.

Walker, N. M., Eardley, W., & Clasper, J. C. (2014).
UK combat-related pelvic junctional vascular injuries 2008–2011: Implications for future intervention. *Injury*, 45 (10):1585-9.

Wedmore, I., McManus, J. G., Pusateri, A. E., & Holcomb, J. B. (2006).
A special report on the chitosan-based hemostatic dressing: Experience in current combat operations. *J Trauma*, 60 (3):655-658.

Willdridge, D., Hodgetts, T., Mahoney, P., & Jarvis, L. (2010).
The Joint Theatre Clinical Case Conference: clinical governance in action. *J R Army Med Corps*, 156 (2):79-83.

Books

BATLS 2008. (2008).
Battlefield Advanced Trauma Life Support (4th edition). Joint Service Publication 570, pp.2 – 3.

Bowden, M. (1999).
Black Hawk Down. London & New York: Bantam Press, pp.209 – 245.

Buckenmaier III, C., & Mahoney, P. (2015a).
Preface., in Buckenmaier, C. I., & Mahoney, P., eds. *Combat Anesthesia: the first 24 hours* Washington - US Army Medical Department: The Borden Institute, p.xxiii. http://www.cs.amedd.army.mil/FileDownloadpublic.aspx?docid=123f6b20-e846-46a6-a2c0-5840a07944c4 (10 July 2015).

Buckenmaier, C. I., & Mahoney, P., eds. (2015b).
Combat Anesthesia: the first 24 hours. Washington - US Army Medical Department: The Borden Institute. http://www.cs.amedd.army.mil/borden/Portlet. aspx?id=4f129d5e-973b-48d9-9fb1-514e6daf90e6 (12 July 2015).

Buckenmaier, C., & Galloway, K. T. (2015).
Combat Trauma Outcomes Tracking and Research. In Buckenmaier, C. I., & Mahoney, P., eds. *Combat Anesthesia: the first 24 hours* Washington - US Army Medical Department: The Borden Institute, pp.275 – 282. http://www.cs.amedd.army.mil/borden/Portlet.aspx?id=4f129d5e-973b-48d9-9fb1-514e6daf90e6 (12 July 2015).

Dannatt. (2013).
Foreword by General the Lord Dannatt, Chief of the General Staff (2006–2009). In C. Froggatt, & B. Adams, *Wounded - the legacy of war* Germany: Steidl, p.13.

Derenelagi, D. (2013).
Private Derek Derenelagi. In C. Froggatt, & B. Adams, *Wounded - The Legacy of War.* Germany: Steidl, pp.186 – 193.

Farrell, T. (2013a).
Army transformation: imperatives and innovations. In T. Farrell, S. Reyning, & T. Terriff, *Transforming military power since the Cold War – Britain, France and the United States, 1991–2012.* Cambridge: Cambridge University Press, pp.1 – 14.

Farrell, T. (2013b).
Introduction: Military Adaptation in War. In T. Farrell, F. Osinga, & J. A. Russell, *Military Adaptation in Afghanistan.* California: Stanford University Press, pp.1 – 23.

Freedman, L. (2013).
The Revolution in Military Affairs. In L. Freedman, *Strategy - A History* (pp.214 – 236). Oxford: Oxford University Press.

Froggatt, C., & Adams, B. (2013).
Wounded - the legacy of war. Germany: Steidl.

Gerhardt, R. T., Mabry, R. L., De Lorenzo, R. A., & Butler, F. K. (2015).
Fundamentals of Combat Casualty Care. Washington - US Army Medical Department: Borden Institute http://www.cs.amedd.army.mil/borden/book/ccc/UCLAchp3.pdf (27 May 2015).

Gray, C. S. (2005).
Another bloody century – Future Warfare London: Wiedenfeld & Nicolson, p.105.

Hodgetts, T., Mahoney, P. F., Evans, G., & Brooks, A. (2005).
Battlefield advanced trauma life support. 3rd edition (BATLS 2005 - Joint Service Publication 570). Defence Medical Education and Training Agency.

Hodgetts, T. J., Clasper, J., Mahoney, P. F., & Russell, R. (2008).
Battlefield Advanced Trauma Life Support - 4th edition, October 2008.
Joint Medical Command: Joint Service Publication 570.

Howard, M., & Paret, P. (2008).
Carl von Clausewitz, On War. Princeton, NJ: Princeton University Press.

Kuhn, T. (1962).
The Structure of Scientific Revolutions. Chicago: University of Chicago Press.

Nessen, S. C., Lounsbury, D. E., & Hetz, S. P. (2008).
War Surgery in Afghanistan and Iraq – A series of cases, 2003 – 2007.
Washington: The Borden Institute.

Parker, C. (2013).
Brigadier Chris Parker CBE QHP. Foreword. In C. Froggatt, & B. Adams,
Wounded — the legacy of war. Germany: Steidl, pp.10 – 11.

Parkinson, B. (2013).
Lance Bombardier Ben Parkinson MBE. In C. Froggatt, & B. Adams,
Wounded - The Legacy of War. Germany: Steidl, pp.78 – 83.

PHTLS. (2005).
Prehospital Trauma Life Support Manual: Military Edition.
5th edition . St Louis, MO: Elsevier Mosby.

Pope, C. D. (2015).
The Medical Emergency Response Team. In Buckenmaier, C. I., & Mahoney, P., eds.
Combat Anesthesia: the first 24 hours. Washington - US Army Medical Department:
The Borden Institute, pp.44 – 46. http://www.cs.amedd.army.mil/borden/
Portlet.aspx?id=4f129d5e-973b-48d9-9fb1-514e6daf90e6 (12 July 2015).

Posen, B. R. (1984).
The Sources of Military Doctrine: France, Britain and Germany between the Wars.
Ithaca NY: Cornell University Press, p.47.

Russell, R., (ed) (2012).
Clinical Guidelines for Operations. Joint Service Publication 999 (3rd edition / Change 3:
September 2012). (This superseded Joint Doctrine Publication 4-03.1 (2010, 2nd edition).

Ministry of Defence, Shrivenham: Development, Concepts and Doctrine Centre
https://www.gov.uk/government/uploads/system/uploads/attachment_data/
file/79106/20121204-8-AVB-CGO_Online_2012.pdf (28 June 2015).

Savitsky, E., & Eastridge, B. (2012).
Combat Casualty Care: Lessons Learned from OEF and OIF. Washington - US Army
Medical Department: The Borden Institute. http://www.cs.amedd.army.mil/borden/
Portlet.aspx?id=a0798abf-8cf0-4af2-9043-86ecd9935057 (20 August 2015).

Stewart, R., & Majada, J. (2014).
Bethune in Spain. Canada: McGill Queen's University Press.

Stringer, A. (2013).
Private Alex Stringer. In C. Froggatt, & B. Adams,
Wounded - The Legacy of War. Germany: Steidl, pp.26 – 35.

Tipping, R. D., MacDermott, S. M., Davis, C., & Carter, T. E. (2015).
Air Transport of the Critical Care Patient. Chapter 38. In C. Buckenmaier III, & P. F. Mahoney,
Combat Anesthesia: The first 24 hours (pp.391 – 399).
Washington DC: US Army Medical Department - The Borden Institute.

Wessely, S. (2013).
The psychological impact of Operations in Iraq: what has it been, and what can we expect in the future?
In J. Bailey, R. Iron, & H. Strachan, *British Generals in Blair's Wars* (Chapter 17, pp.201 – 212).
Surrey: Ashgate.

PhD Dissertation

Hodgetts, T. (2012a).
A revolutionary approach to improving combat casualty care. (Unpublished Doctoral thesis, City University London) http://openaccess.city.ac.uk/2040/ (15 January 2015).

Reports and Directives

Allied Joint Publication-4.10(B) (NATO Standard, Edition B, Version 1 with UK National Elements, published 28 July 2015). (2015).

Allied Joint Doctrine for Medical Support. (Ministry of Defence: Development, Concepts and Doctrine Centre, Shrivenham). https://www.gov.uk/government/uploads/system/uploads/attachment_data/file/454625/20150708-nato_ajp_4_10_uk_secured.pdf (accessed 20 August 2015).

CADTH. (2014).
Junctional Tourniquets for controlling haemorrhage from wounds in adults: a review of clinical effectiveness, cost-effectiveness, safety, and guidelines. CADTH Rapid Response Report: Summary with critical appraisal, 10 April 2014. Ottawa (ON): Canadian Agency for Drugs and Technologies in Health. pp.1 – 12. http://www.ncbi.nlm.nih.gov/books/NBK269192/pdf/Bookshelf_NBK269192.pdf (28 June 2015).

CBIS. (2015).
Annual Report 2014. London, March 2015 http://imperial.ac.uk/blastinjurystudies (25 June 2015).

Davis, P. R., Griffiths, A., & Nadin, M. N. (2006).
Delivering Tactical Pre-hospital Critical Care - The Medical Emergency Response Team (A paper by 16 Close Support Medical Regiment, 1 October 2006). Internal Defence Paper.

Defense Health Board (2015).
Combat Trauma Lessons Learned from Military Operations of 2001 – 2013 Report (published 9 March 2015) http://www.health.mil/Reference-Center/Reports/2015/03/09/Combat-Trauma-Lessons-Learned-from-Military-Operations (20 August 2015)

Defence Statistics (Health). (2015).
Ministry of Defence: Quarterly Afghanistan and Iraq Amputation Statistics, 7 October 2001 – 31 March 2015 (Abbey Wood, Bristol: 30 April 2015). https://www.gov.uk/government/statistics/uk-service-personnel-amputations-financial-year-201415 (20 June 2015).

Director General Medical Operational Capability Report. (2006).
Defence Medical Services.

Gilbert, P. (2010).
Post Operational Report OP HERRICK 11A, Joint Force Medical Group, Role 3 Hospital Squadron, (256 (City of London) Field Hospital (Volunteers), dated 28 February 2010.

Gilbert, S. (2013).
Improving the survivability of NATO ground forces. NATO Parliamentary Assembly – Annual Report 2013, Science and Technology Committee, 13 October 2013, www.nato-pa.int (25 July 2015).

Graham, D. (2011).
Post-Operational Interview, 17 June 2011 (quoted in: Chapter 4-2 Health Service Support, in: The HERRICK Campaign Study (Army Briefing Note, 27 February 2015), p.4-2_1.

Healthcare Commission Report. (2009).
A review of the clinical governance of the Defence Medical Services in the UK and overseas. March 2009:13–17. http://www.nhs.uk/NHSEngland/Militaryhealthcare/Documents/Defence_Medical_Services_review[1].pdf. (20 October 2014)

Hodgetts, T. J., Parkhouse, H., & Cobb, B. (1998).
Major Trauma Clinical Effectiveness Project, Annual report 1997-1998.

Hodgetts, T., Turner, L., Grieves, T., & Payne, S. (2000b).
Major Trauma: Report of clinical effectiveness on Operation Agricola (Kosovo 1999). Defence Logistics Organisation.

House of Commons Defence Committee. (1999).
Seventh Report. The Strategic Defence Review: Defence Medical Services - Background. The Stationery Office: London.

House of Commons Defence Committee. (2011).
Advances in medical care resulting in more personnel surviving injuries. In *The Armed Forces Covenant in Action? Part 1: Military Casualties, (HC 762). Seventh Report of*

Session 2010–12 (p.15, Q310). London: The Stationery Office http://www.parliament.uk/business/committees/committees-a-z/commons-select/defence-committee/inquiries/parliament-2010/the-military-covenant-in-action-part-1-military-casualies/ (8 March 2015).

House of Commons Defence Committee. (2012).
The Armed Forces Covenant in Action? Part 1: Military Casualties: Government Response to the Committee's Seventh Report of Session 2010–12. London: The Stationery Office, p.4 http://www.publications.parliament.uk/pa/cm201012/cmselect/cmdfence/1855/1855.pdf (24 July 2015).

Marshall, A. W. (1993).
Some thoughts on Military Revolutions. *Memorandum for the Record*, (pp.1-8). Office of the Secretary of Defense - Office of Net Assessment, July 27, 1993.

National Audit Office. (2010).
Ministry of Defence: Treating Injury and Illness arising on Military Operations. http://www.nao.org.uk/wp-content/uploads/2010/02/0910294.pdf (20 January 2015).

NATO. (2010).
Allied Command Operations - Directive for Medical Support to Operations: Promoting Excellence in Healthcare Support on Operations. NATO AD 83-1 (2e).

Operational Patient Care Pathway. (2014).
Ministry of Defence: Joint Service Publication (JSP) 950 Leaflet 1-4-1. https://www.gov.uk/government/publications/operational-patient-care-pathway (1 March 2015).

Operational Patient Care Pathway (Figures). (2014).
Operational Patient Care Pathway. *Annex B to To HQ SG/29-08-33 Dated 21 Jul 14.* https://www.gov.uk/government/uploads/system/uploads/attachment_data/file/377889/20140721-Operational_Patient_Care_Pathway_JSP_950_AnnexB_Ed2_Final.pdf (3 August 2015).

PTSD Class Action. (2003).
Multiple Claimants v The Ministry of Defence (Part 1) [2003] EWHC 1134 (QB) (21 May 2003). (p. Paragraph 5.116). http://www.bailii.org/ew/cases/EWHC/QB/2003/1134.html (29 June 2015).

Surgeon General's Policy Letter. (2007)
https://www.gov.uk/government/groups/defence-medical-services#surgeon-general (28 June 2015).

Newspaper articles

Farmer, B. (2015, June 2).
Medical advances saw 38 troops live through 'un-survivable' injuries in Iraq and Afghanistan. *The Daily Telegraph*, http://www.telegraph.co.uk/news/uknews/defence/11646952/Medical-advances-saw-38-troops-live-through-un-survivable-injuries-in-Iraq-and-Afghanistan.html (14 June 2015).

Grice, E. (2010, January 19).
Hi-tech prosthetics are getting our injured back on their feet. *The Daily Telegraph*.

Websites

BASICS. *Brigadier Ian Haywood (obituary)*
http://www.basics.org.uk/about_us/imc_greats/haywood_bio (accessed 5 July 2015).

British Army. (2014).
Final tour in Afghanistan for hospital medics, 23 April 2014.
http://www.army.mod.uk/news/26241.aspx (2 January 2015).

British Army.
Casualty Care
http://www.army.mod.uk/welfare-support/23238.aspx (25 July 2015)

Centre for Blast Injury Studies (Imperial College London)
http://www.imperial.ac.uk/blast-injury/ (28 June 2015)

CIOMR (Interallied Confederation of Medical Reserve Officers).
Battlefield Advanced Trauma Life Support (BATLS)
http://ciomr.org/service/resources/militmilitary-trauma-care/battlefield-advanced-trauma-life-support-batls (12 August 2015).

Doughty, H. (2014).
Blood Brothers. (live broadcast onTEDxBrum, 8 November 2014)
https://www.ted.com/tedx/events/12748 , also https://www.youtube.
com/watch?v=QxaYzFAJY_0 ; (both accessed 15 June 2015).

Etherington, J. (2014).
The Work of the Defence Medical Rehabilitation Centre, Headley Court – Gresham
College Lecture, 24 March 2014. http://www.gresham.ac.uk/lectures-and-events/the-
work-of-the-defence-medical-rehabilitation-centre-headley-court (3 August 2015).

JRAMC (Journal of the Royal Army Medical Corps). Many of the lessons and
advances in combat casualty care from Iraq and Afghanistan as well as other
conflicts have been captured in articles, campaign reports, and special supplements
of the Journal of the Royal Army Medical Corps. As of February 2020, this
Journal has become BMJ Military Health. https://militaryhealth.bmj.com

KCMHR and ADMMH publications, King's College London
http://www.kcl.ac.uk/kcmhr/pubdb (7 July 2015).

MOD Press Office. (2015).
Study shows dramatic improvement in survival rates for battlefield casualties.
30 May 2015 https://modmedia.blog.gov.uk/2015/05/30/study-shows-dramatic-
improvement-in-survival-rates-for-battlefield-casualties/ (14 June 2015).

Military Anaesthesia.
http://www.niaa.org.uk/Military-Anaesthesia (29 June 2015).

Oxford Dictionary. (2015).
Oxford: Oxford University Press
http://www.oxforddictionaries.com/definition/english/paradigm (1 March 2015).

Parker, C. (2013).
The revolution in battlefield medicine and healthcare for the wounded
(Interview with Brigadier Chris Parker 18 April 2013). Institute for International
Strategic Studies. https://www.iiss.org/en/events/events/archive/2013-5126/
july-bdc1/revolution-in-battlefield-medicine-18d1 (28 June 2015).

Poulter, D. (2013).
£11 million funding boost to improve NHS care for war veterans.
(15 February 2013) https://www.gov.uk/government/news/11-million-
funding-boost-to-improve-nhs-care-for-war-veterans (5 August 2015).

Swansea University. (2010).
MSc Trauma Surgery (Military). http://www.swansea.ac.uk/postgraduate/taught/
medicine/msc-trauma-surgery-military/#key-features=is-expanded (10 July 2015).

Annex - British Field Hospital Deployments to Iraq and Afghanistan, 2001 – 2014

	Iraq - Op TELIC 1-13	Afghanistan - Op HERRICK 4-20 Camp Bastion Hospital
22 Field Hospital	Op TELIC 1 (Feb – May 03) Op TELIC 3 (Nov 03–May 04) Op TELIC 8 (May–Oct 06) (RHQ & Support Squadron) Op TELIC 13 (Dec 08–Apr 09)	Op HERRICK 4 (Apr–Sep 06) (Hospital Squadron) Op HERRICK 16 (Apr–Oct 12)
33 Field Hospital	Op TELIC 1 (Feb–May 03) Op TELIC 2 (Jul–Nov 03) Op TELIC 5 (Nov 04–Apr 05) Op TELIC 9 (Nov 06–May 07)	Op HERRICK 11 (Oct 09–Apr 10) Op HERRICK 18 (Apr–Oct 13)
34 Field Hospital	Op TELIC 1 (Feb–May 03) Op TELIC 7 (Nov 05–Apr 06) Op TELIC 10 (May–Nov 07)	Op FINGAL (Dec 01–May 02) (Bagram, North Afghanistan) Op HERRICK 12 (Apr–Oct 10) Op HERRICK 20 (Apr–Sep 14)
201 Field Hospital		Op HERRICK 7A (Nov 07–Jan 08) Op HERRICK 15B (Jan–Apr 12)
202 Field Hospital	Op TELIC 1 (Feb–May 03)	Op HERRICK 10A (Apr–Jul 09) Op HERRICK 19B (Jan–Apr 14)
203 Field Hospital		Op HERRICK 8A (May–Jul 08) Op HERRICK 19A (Oct 13–Jan 14)
204 Field Hospital		Op HERRICK 8B (Jul–Oct 08) Op HERRICK 17B (Jan–Apr 13)
205 Field Hospital	Op TELIC 6 (May–Nov 05)	Op HERRICK 11B (Jan–Apr 10)
207 Field Hospital	Op TELIC 4A (May–Aug 04)	Op HERRICK 13A (Oct 10–Jan 11)
208 Field Hospital		Op HERRICK 6B (Jul–Oct 07) Op HERRICK 15A (Oct 11–Jan 12)
212 Field Hospital		Op HERRICK 6A (May–Jul 07) Op HERRICK 13B (Jan–Apr 11)
243 Field Hospital		Op HERRICK 7B (Jan–Apr 08) Op HERRICK 17A (Oct 12–Jan 13)
256 Field Hospital	Op TELIC 4B (Aug–Nov 04)	Op HERRICK 11A (Oct 09–Jan 10)
RAF Hospital Squadron	Op TELIC 8 (May–Oct 06)	
Royal Navy Hospital Squadron		Op HERRICK 5 (Oct 06–Apr 07) Op HERRICK 9 (Nov 08–Apr 09) Op HERRICK 14 (Apr–Oct 11)
Danish Field Hospital		Op HERRICK 10B (Jul–Nov 09)
1 Close Support Medical Regiment (provided Hospital Squadron)	Op TELIC 11	
3 Close Support Medical Regiment (provided Hospital Squadron)	Op TELIC 12	